PURPLE
FLAT TOP

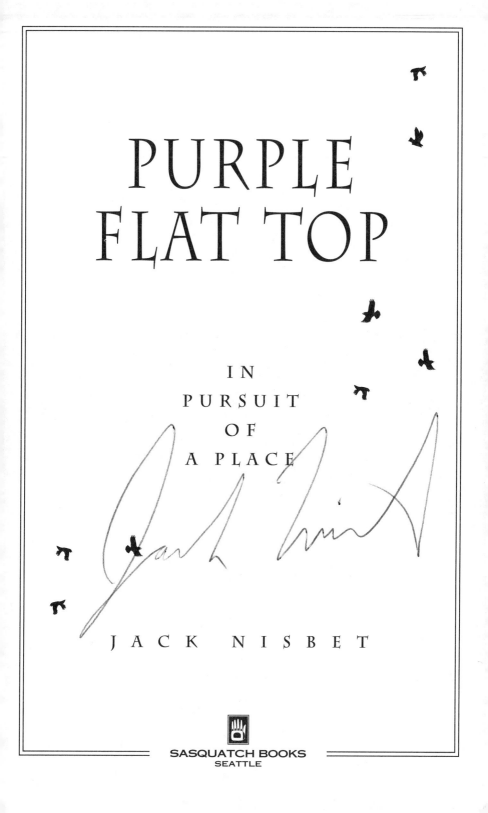

PURPLE
FLAT TOP

IN
PURSUIT
OF
A PLACE

JACK NISBET

SASQUATCH BOOKS
SEATTLE

Printed in the United States of America.

Some of the stories in this collection appeared, in different forms, in *Sky People* (Quartzite Books, 1984).

Cover and interior design: Rohani Design, Edmonds, WA
Cover photograph: M. Michaelae McKay Larkin
Interior illustrations and map: Michael Rohani

Library of Congress Cataloging in Publication Data

Nisbet, Jack, 1949–
    Purple Flat Top : in search of a place / Jack Nisbet.
        p. m.
    ISBN 1-57061-058-4
    1. Chewelah Region (Wash.)—Social life and customs. 2. Nisbet,
Jack, 1949– 3. Natural history—Washington—Chewelah Region.
I. Title.
F899.C525N57   1996
979.7'23—dc20   95-52137

Sasquatch Books
1008 Western Avenue
Seattle, Washington 98104
(206)467-4300

CONTENTS

*E*xcept for a few compressions of time and name changes, these are works of nonfiction. My sincere appreciation goes out to all the people involved.

Dedicated to teachers no longer with us: Carolina Beck, Fay Bristol, Klaus Lackshewitz, Shirley LaMont, Selena Garry Pascal, Babe Reynolds, and Jan Triplett.

Special thanks to Al Bartell for naming the place, and to Leo and Hazel Beck, Lillian Bennett, the Bristol family, Walt Goodman, John LaMont, and Noreen Paulson.

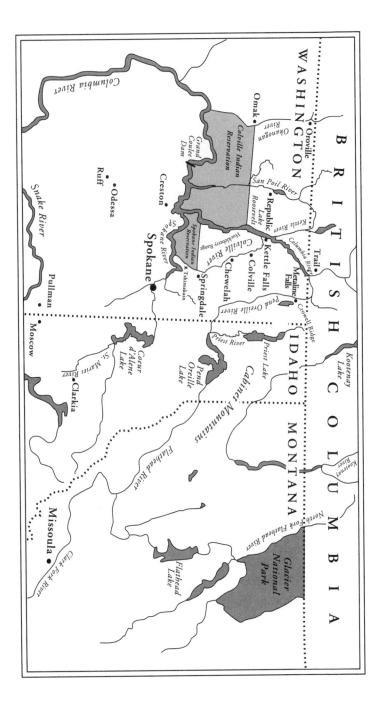

PURPLE FLAT TOP

WE WERE HALFWAY AROUND THE curve when I spotted an overgrown dirt road branching off to the left. Tom saw it at the same time and swung up its steep incline. At the top of the hill the track leveled out abruptly, and my head banged against the roof as we dropped into a deep rut. Branches from spindly pines slapped at the sides of the car and poked through our open windows. As Tom slowed for a dip, I glanced for the hundredth time at our dog-eared set of directions. They had sounded easy enough when we set out from the Spokane airport: drive fifty miles north on Highway 395; go straight through the town of Chewelah; turn right on a gravel county road, then left on a Jeep trail. That would lead to a distinctive rock outcrop called Purple Flat Top; a survey marker beneath a big pine snag would tell us we were in the right place for certain.

Neither of us had been anywhere near this part of northeastern Washington before. We were here on a spring jaunt from college, planning to camp out on a remote piece of land owned by Tom's dad. But the roads weren't matching up very well with our map, and for the last day and a half we had squeezed our rented Volkswagen Bug down a whole series of blind Jeep trails to visit a whole succession of rough outcrops and dead conifers. We backtracked to Chewelah to ask for help, but when we told people we were trying to find a place called Purple Flat Top, they looked at us like we were crazy.

"Purple Flat Head?" a man at the hardware store said. "What's that?"

As we bumped along our latest overgrown track, feeling a little foolish, a break in the trees revealed a scree slope ascending into a rough headland of vertical cliffs. At a small clearing the road skirted a boulder pile, then forked. Tom stopped the car and we clambered out to investigate. To our right a jumble of rocks marched uphill toward the blunt shoulder of the escarpment; to our left a brushy slope bursting with serviceberry and hawthorn blooms fell away to a noisy creek far below. A line of high mare's tail clouds raced across the sky, and everything about the place seemed sharp and new. We bushwhacked down the slope to a grassy bench that overlooked the clear-running stream. Off in the trees stood a monstrous lightning-struck pine snag, and we clawed through a tangle of wild roses to sweep through the needles at its base.

"Look," Tom said, leaning back to show me a brass survey cap planted in the ground. Stamped into its face were the township and section numbers we had been looking for.

We whooped with satisfaction, then stood up with arms spread at right angles to gauge the boundaries of the property. A short scramble returned us to the base of the cliffs, where a mound of raw, fist-sized fragments stood out among the slide of rocky talus. We kicked around among the shattered stones and soon found a hole the diameter of a silver dollar neatly drilled into one toe of the outcrop. Nearby, bits of faded blue and yellow wire confirmed that there had been blasting here. That would have been back in 1955, when Tom's father, Fay Bristol, had taken an interest in this property. After the assay tested out at ninety-nine percent quartzite, he bought 160 acres around the cliffs, then spent the next fifteen years busily mining slightly purer ore in other places.

From the blast site, Tom and I traced the rough boundary line uphill. A lattice of deer paths wound between stubby outcrops and stunted yellow pines, through loose rocks that ranged in color from the pink and yellow of bull quartz to burnt red and orange and fawn brown. As we worked our way through the rash of wildflowers that dappled the rocky ground, a late afternoon sun pulled a warm translucence from the stones, and the cliffs took on a rosy purple glow. It was this tone that Fay's partner must have spotted from the window of his small plane in the early fifties, inspiring him to scribble "Purple Flat Top" on his map.

When we reached the top, huffing a bit, we found ourselves on a plateau that dipped and rose behind a steep precipice. In the fresh breeze we crouched as close to the edge as we dared. A single raven floated just below us. The jet black bird traced the long curve of crumbling stacks, then disappeared around a jagged pinnacle without once flapping its wings. Outward from the cliffs the sea of purple scree spread onto the forested bench. A wide, glaciated valley opened out beyond, where the puny Colville River wound through patterns of green fields and black plowed earth. Gently rounded hills surrounded the valley, their hard-scraped faces testifying to the passage of ice. Directly east of

us a massive cleaved monolith, far grander than Purple Flat
Top, towered over the town of Chewelah. A wooden grain
elevator and the ruins of some defunct industrial operation
flanked the highway south to Spokane.

Looking out over the valley, we returned to the subject
that had lured us here, the idea of building a cabin out in the
woods. Tom was an architecture student, itching to con-
struct something of his own design. This seemed like a
perfect place, and he was sure his dad would let us have a go
at it. That suited me just fine—working outside for the
summer, in a place full of strange plants and animals, was
exactly what I wanted to do.

Anxious to explore more of the land, we planned our
attack while making a quick descent. At the wide talus pile
near the bottom, the rocks spilled out in a colorful spray,
ranging in size from fists to bread loaves to fruit boxes. Their
weathered surfaces were decorated with black and green
lichens, and some were shot through with veins of pure
white quartz. When flung back down on the pile, each one
threw off fresh sparks and the smell of close lightning. It
didn't take us long to decide that our cabin belonged on the
open bench by the marker snag, and that we should build it
out of this wonderful stone. The fact that neither of us had
more than a passing acquaintance with a mason's trowel only
spurred us on.

That June, filled with anticipation, we coasted into the
Colville Valley in our newly acquired '55 Chevy pickup. On
the grassy point above the creek, we swept a pack rat nest out
of the crude assay shack that Fay Bristol had left behind, and
Tom set up a drawing board inside, so that he could draft a set
of working plans for our cabin. "Now," he said, "I guess we'd
better find out if there's any good water around."

I had grown up in the Carolinas. When my father built a
house, he picked a site with a view, then simply sank a well

beside it. Water problems for us consisted of muddy roads and leaky basements. But things were different out West, Tom insisted. Water was the whole thing here.

"Maybe we can get Dad up to help us," he suggested.

Fay Bristol was a big, loose-jointed man, dressed in pea green slacks and a pair of Pendleton shirts. He looked a little worn out by the drive from Portland but began to wake up as he inspected the old blast site at the base of Purple Flat Top.

"You know, I've scrambled all over up there," he said.

He stuck his nose into the assay shack, then crashed into the brush to slice off a willow twig a couple of feet long. With a small pocketknife he peeled the greenish yellow bark back from one end, then balanced the finger-sized shoot on his forefinger. The tip of his tongue crept out of the left side of his mouth, and the witching began.

Fay rambled along a random path, muttering and chewing his tongue as he searched this way and that for indicator trees. The willow dowsing stick bounced along his fingers like a weightless spring. Every once in a while his whole body shook as if from an electric shock; he would stop, point to the ground, and call for a mark. While Tom and I tried to keep up with hatchet and stakes, Fay's mutterings grew into a narration of the story beneath the ground.

"Here it is, off this way now. See that maple clump? That's the course, but it's just a trickle. Here it collects a little bit, you could get a couple gallons a minute at sixteen feet right here. Now another vein joins in—you'll get your two gallons plus another three or four at thirty. Stake this one here. Wait now . . . it feels like these courses are joining together and running off this way, weaker now, curving with the bank. Let's back up (shake, shake) . . . yeah. This is your best bet so far. I think the two veins combined would give you enough water. Unless you want to try down in that gully."

I had never seen anything like it. Fay and his stick wagged off through the brush again, checking the gully, delineating an invisible system of water that flowed beneath the soil. He knew his geology and clearly described how a block fault had shoved the quartzite up and over the valley's dolomitic lime-stone. But there was an abstract quality to his vision as well.

"It's just seeing in another dimension," Fay explained as he struggled back up the slope. "Pretend there's a lake under the ground here. Now you probably can't tell me a thing about it, but I can see how deep it is, and what direction it flows."

I looked at Tom, who acted like people talked to him this way all the time.

"A lake?" I asked.

Fay stopped for a minute. "Look," he said. "It takes a feel for it, and practice, too. When I was a boy picking peaches in Michigan we had to learn how to work fast, but the bosses wouldn't put up with any green or bruised fruit. So you felt each one just so"—and here Fay cupped his hand around the air, as if his skin still tingled with a recognition of ripeness. "After you did it a few thousand times, you knew exactly what you were picking. Or at least I did."

A couple of hours of up-and-down walking had com-pletely crumpled both of Fay's shirts, and his face sagged like a worn-out coon hound's. He told us that our best building site lay some way down the bench from our lightning-struck snag, beneath a hillside shaded by Douglas fir and tamarack. We'd be smart, he suggested, to begin by pushing in a new road. Tom showed him a foundation plan he had drawn up for our intended cabin. Fay didn't have any quarrel with the drawing, but he didn't see why we wanted to use the pink quartzite.

"You know better than this, Tom. This isn't building stone here, it's too sharp. You can't shape quartzite with a hammer."

Tom said we thought we could lay them up so they looked good.

"We'll find out soon enough," Fay responded. "It's kind of like dowsing. Some people have a feel for masonry, and some don't. You hand a couple guys a trowel and then you go away for a while. When you come back, there's a wall there and you either say 'OK,' or you say, 'Oh no,'" Fay shook his large head back and forth, jowls flapping, " 'why don't you tear this goddamned thing down?' "

With that, Fay was done. Tom and I drove him back to his car in downtown Chewelah, gratefully accepted his offer of a steak dinner, and watched him head off into the long summer evening.

There was plenty of daylight left as we rattled back down the dirt road below the cliffs, so we stopped to visit the site Fay had found. It seemed dark and close, and after an uneasy half hour we returned to the assay shack. The grassy point basked in the last rays of the day, and in the distance we could trace the long ridge of the Huckleberry Mountains running north. Tom turned his back on the sunset and walked over behind the assay shack, where a tangle of alders and willows surrounded the puddle of an old spring. Fay had cut his dowsing stick from the greenery that morning, but when we asked him if the spring would serve as a water source, he responded with a quick shrug.

"Surface runoff. Some farmer probably dug it out to try and water his cows. You can't depend on anything like that."

Now Tom and I surveyed the spring again. The clumps of willow and alder that draped over the murky puddle were obviously thriving. Deer pellets decorated clumps of mint and nettle. Surely there had to be a steady flow to support this kind of life.

"I don't know about Dad's spot," Tom said, shaking his head. "He just cares about water. But I still think we have the best place right here. Maybe we can make something out of this little spring."

We spent the next two days digging blue mud out of the puddle. When the raw sides started to cave, we sharpened a bunch of two-by-six stakes, drove them down in a rough ring, and kept shoveling. At a depth of about five feet, gravel of several sizes combined with the gummy clay to make progress painfully slow. When we couldn't dig anymore, we rolled a section of steel highway culvert up the slope and turned it upright in the hole. A couple feet of water rose inside it right away. We plumbed a length of plastic pipe into the bottom of our casing, ran it downhill to a showerhead tacked to a tree, and thought we had it made.

For the rest of the summer we scoured the base of Purple Flat Top for square cornerstones and the flattest, most colorful faces. Each morning we would hoe up a batch of mortar in a long wooden box, then lay the precious stones one by one, picking and choosing from the vast selection we had spread around the grassy point. We wiped the joints smooth with gloved fingers and swept the day's work clean with a whisk broom. Every evening, without fail, we stood back and admired the growing puzzle of our stonework.

I fell asleep each night to a chorus of coyotes on the hill above, and jumped up in the morning with the first babble of jake brakes from logging trucks on the high road across the creek. Then I would listen to the croaks and boinks of waking ravens while I looked for good building stones and anything else I could find. Wild clematis and pink bitterroot cropped up among the rocks, rubber boas and blue-tailed skinks beneath them. I learned to recognize the songs of redstarts and lazuli buntings, and once I stumbled upon a veery's nest, tucked neatly between a ninebark bush and a table-sized slab of quartzite.

As summer wore on, it stopped raining altogether, and the world dried up around us. Glacial dust boiled through the Chevy's leaky vents, and our noses stayed plugged day and night. Lightning strikes ignited forest fires all over Stevens County that August, casting a thick yellow pall that obscured the sun. With the dry weather came hoards of yellowjackets, which kept us hopping and swatting through every meal on our eating porch. Then the water in our culvert dropped below the level of the outlet pipe, so that we had to lean in and dip it out by the bucketful.

September arrived, and it was time for us to return to school. The morning we left, there was frost on the dust, and the walls of our cabin were not quite two feet high all the way around.

Tom and I returned for the next two summers to add courses to the stone work, and eventually we were ready for the roof. The walls curved and wobbled a little, but we were awfully proud of them. In the process of building the cabin, we had become acquainted with half the people in the Colville Valley, and figured we could make a living with a modest contracting business. Our presence here had taken on a permanence that neither of us had anticipated; the possibilities of a second house, hot showers, and a gravel driveway began to enter our conversations. The problem was that late every summer the water level in our spring box sank out of sight, leaving us to lug buckets up from the creek or haul barrelfuls from town. If we were really going to live below the cliffs year-round, we had to shape up our water system.

On the ridge behind Purple Flat Top, perhaps two miles from the cliffs and several hundred feet above the elevation of our bench, lay the remains of an abandoned homestead. Big cottonwood trees surrounded the fallen-in house, and irises and lilacs still bloomed each spring. Most impressive to us was a gnarled orchard that covered several rolling acres; every time we went there, we wondered why anyone would abandon such a fruitful place.

The water supply for this entire spread was a hand-dug sidehill spring, much like our own just down the hill. The homesteaders had built a low rock wall to create a cistern, and two grand firs, a tamarack, and a clump of vine maple sprouted beside the small pond. Bright songbirds always hung around in the luxurious shade. One dry afternoon, when Tom and I went up to gather pears and apples from the deserted orchard, we stopped to marvel at the water lapping against those crudely laid stones.

"Look how these guys made it work," Tom said. "What if we dig our spring out deeper? We could line it with concrete and make ourselves a cistern even bigger than this one. Get a backhoe in and really ream it out."

Jerry Pope was a fast-working backhoe operator, chunky and wire-haired, who winked each time he spoke to one of us. It turned out that Jerry knew something about water, too—enough to tell us we shouldn't just dig blind, even though there might be moisture showing at the surface of our spring. Jerry said he had some feeling for a stick himself, and since we obviously had a head start on things, he would gladly check to make sure.

Jumping down from his tractor with a wink, he used a hatchet to hack a forked stick from a nearby alder and began to pace back and forth around our spring. His two-handed style was much more determined than Fay's light-fingered bounces, but the two men shared the same hurried agitation.

On a level spot just below the spring, Jerry's stick twisted strongly down.

"That's her," he said, rocking up on his toes to congratulate himself. "There's water right here. And it'll be a heck of a lot easier to set those rings here than up on that muddy slope."

Tom and I were excited now. We urged Jerry on, barely able to stand clear of his wildly swinging hoe as he dug the hole. Little seeps of water showed from six feet on, and at about fourteen feet Jerry's steel bucket clunked against bedrock. Before lunchtime, he had cleaned off the hard stone, used his loader to stack up four sections of concrete culvert, and backfilled around the cylinder. When we peered down through the top ring and wondered why there was only the barest hint of wetness at the bottom, Jerry shook his head and winked: "No worry. It'll rise up in an hour or two."

He spent the rest of the afternoon digging a network of ditches from the new hole to the house and back out to our proposed drain field. Tom and I would watch his backhoe work for a while, then wander over to our new concrete hole. With a flashlight we could see that the bottom was still damp, but not even an optimist could measure a change of depth. We were creating a very elaborate flow system for water that wasn't rising.

It was late in the day before our thirty-two-dollar-an-hour panic convinced Jerry to get off his machine and take a look.

"Huh," he mumbled, gazing into the empty cistern. "Must have gotten lost somewhere."

When he returned the next morning, we gathered around the stacked culverts and stared down to their damp bottom. Jerry voiced the theory that it might take the water a few days to rise. Tom shook his head and looked up the slope at the original spring.

Jerry removed the concrete rings, set them off in the woods, and filled in his diggings of the previous day. Then we worked late into the evening with garden rakes, trying to smooth out the mess. By dusk our place looked like a trenched battle scene. We were flat out of money, and our water supply still consisted of one salvaged culvert stuck in an old stock watering hole.

A few months later we decided to try again, but we had no intention of repeating the anxiety of our dry hole day. This time we would ask for professional help. A neighbor gave us the name of Al Lang. When I phoned, he said sure, he would drive down—always interested in a search for water.

Al arrived after a full day's work at his state job up in Colville. He was a mild, slender man in his early thirties with heavy-framed glasses and a dispassionate voice. With a black pocketknife, he sliced off a forked maple branch, explaining as he whittled that he never charged for his services and never guaranteed that he was right.

"This witching business is just a feeling that some people have. It takes a lot of practice to read the pulls on the stick."

Al said he was always happy to learn more about what might be happening under the ground; he felt that he could judge surface water fairly well, and read different veins and flows accurately down to around thirty feet. After that the sensations got kind of vague, and the only way he knew to home in on the flow was to follow it out.

"I always try to check back at the places where I do some work," he said, "to see how the water holds up."

We took Al down to our trial sump and described our frantic day with Jerry's backhoe. Approaching his task like an accountant circling a suspicious set of ledgers, Al walked slowly back and forth, showing no trace of the adrenaline that had fueled Fay's and Jerry's attempts. After a careful survey of the area, Al allowed that we had the right idea and that, as far as he could tell, Jerry had dug only ten feet to the left of a pretty good seam.

"Yeah, I know it seems off the natural line," he said. "But I feel some water here at six feet, and at thirteen there's more. It might run slow at first, but you know what they say: the more you use it, the better she flows."

Tom and I nodded hesitantly.

"Why don't you get a second opinion before you dig?" suggested Al. "Try old Fritz Wilde. He might charge you twenty bucks, but I hear he's pretty good. Put on a show for you, anyhow."

A couple of weeks later, as Tom and I were trying to fit a window into a hole that was slightly out of square, a battered sedan appeared in the driveway. When I approached the car, a leather-faced man leaped away from the driver's seat and barked at the cliffs.

"Don't come near me. Don't say a word. If it's water you want, I'll find it myself. Not a hint from anyone!"

Fritz sniffed the air, then leaned into the back seat of his dusty Plymouth and emerged with a pair of stainless steel refrigerator rods. The rods were bent at right angles, and he gripped them like three-foot pistols. He straightened again and laughed maniacally.

"Not a word now," he said, focusing on the ends of his glistening rods.

The twin pieces of steel wavered, crossed, then turned in unison back toward Fay's old assay shack, which was down a slope and hidden away in the trees.

"We're on the beam now," cackled Fritz, tumbling down into the trees as if he couldn't control the drag of the rods.

Fritz spent the afternoon crossing and recrossing the slope around the spring and the bench below. He talked as he moved, spinning out tales of obscure watercourses discovered during his forty years at the calling. With only a difference of a foot here and a gallon there, he confirmed everything Al Lang had told us.

The more Fritz blustered through the wide range of elements he was used to dowsing—well water, broken pipelines, oil, hard-rock minerals—the more my attention began to wander. He abruptly broke his line of talk and marched straight up to me, thrusting his stainless steel rods against my chest. I played with them for a moment, trying to get the feel, before he spun me around by my shoulders and directed me over the black plastic hose that ran to our shower. The two rods, held loosely in my hands, began to move. Slowly, clumsily, they crossed. My hands began to sweat on the polished steel.

"Everybody's got it, only some more than others," Fritz remarked, as I stared at the two rods waving back and forth in front of my face. "You can feel the pull, but it's a matter of interpreting the feel. Now, I'm practiced at it and like to look for different things. Has anybody ever tried witching that pile of quartz up there for a little gold?"

We saved our money for more digging, and when we came up short, Tom cashed in his Mercury dime collection. Late in the spring, we called Jerry Pope back for another attempt. This time when he reached a depth of thirteen feet, water bubbled right up to ground level, and once again Tom and I thought we had it made. Water lines and gardening plans quickly fell into place, and Jerry piled lots of dirt beside new ditches.

Then the days of powdery dust returned. By mid-September the water in our cistern sank ten feet, until we could barely see liquid deep down in the bottom. We phoned Al Lang, who assured us that the water table always dropped in the fall.

"It'll come back up, don't worry. Just hope for a lot of snow in the mountains this winter."

We carried bucketfuls of water up from the creek, and waited for some clouds to crawl into the clear blue expanse above Purple Flat Top.

MILK RUN

*T*HAT WAS THE WINTER OUR NEIGHBOR
Lynn Walker finally decided to do something about
his hemorrhoids.

"Why go on?" he asked. "Dairying twenty-three years. Hardly
kept up the interest on my place payment. Why keep choring
when it hurts? I'm gonna let that doctor fix 'em."

Lynn was a bit past forty and still sported the faded jeans
and wiry build of his Montana cowboy upbringing. We were
sitting at his kitchen table, a familiar parking spot for Tom
and me. The Walkers' farm lay on the opposite side of Purple
Flat Top from our place; they were the first family we met
when we arrived in Stevens County, and the first one we
traded favors with. Lynn and his wife, Donna, kept us enter-
tained with their droll estimation of the local scene, and
their connections around town helped us feel our way into
the community.

Lynn was farming two hundred hilly acres, trying to raise enough alfalfa, barley, and oats to feed his small dairy herd through the winter. As soon as he found out that I could drive a tractor, he had me out harrowing the back forty. I liked working for Lynn; his fields rolled up from the valley and wrapped around the foot of Purple Flat Top, and from my seat on his little Case tractor the view was always changing. It wasn't long before I had worn a path from our place along the bottom of the cliffs, past a seep that was often ripe with bear sign, through a neck of woods, and across the open pasture below Lynn's barn. One hop over a strand of electric fence landed me in his yard, and if Lynn wasn't out wrenching on a piece of disassembled equipment, I was sure to find him in the kitchen, ready to spin out the news of the day.

But during the fall I had noticed that he was squirming uncomfortably on the tractor seat, and his complaints about dairying had increased to a steady chorus. On this particular visit he seemed subdued, almost thoughtful. He pushed back his hat and scratched his thinning hair, then glanced out the window at the snow-covered barnyard and farm machinery. It was the week before Christmas, and he was trying to hire Tom and me to milk for him while he was recuperating.

"It'll be easy," he assured us as we all sipped at cups of holiday cheer. He flicked his Marlboro onto his blue jeans, then carefully rubbed the ash into the fabric. "Even if something does go wrong, I'll be right here to help."

This was Tom's and my first full winter in Stevens County, and we hadn't made much progress on our house since the weather turned cold. We had gotten the roof on and the floor planking down, but cloudy plastic shrouded the windows, and the inside was still an empty shell. Sawdust covered every ledge and sill. We were burning through firewood at an alarming rate, but the thick stone walls kept the air inside damp and clammy. On bad days it was like living in a medieval ruin.

From the Walkers' sunlit kitchen we surveyed the layout of Lynn's barnyard. A long milking parlor ran down one side of the big red barn, with a concrete block milkhouse added on the front. Two chicken coops served as calf pens and storage sheds. Lynn and Donna's old-fashioned white farmhouse overlooked an expanse of the Colville Valley, and he liked to brag that the good southern exposure—on the morning side of Purple Flat Top—had allowed the original homesteaders to raise cantaloupes and strawberries right in the front yard. On short winter days, the barnyard was open and bright; it stayed much warmer here than around our shadowy house in the woods. Tom and I looked back and forth from each other to Lynn and nodded at the chance for a change.

Lynn checked into the hospital right after New Year's, so close to the solstice that both morning and evening chores took place entirely in the dark. Tom and I were familiar with the milking parlor because Lynn had pressed us into service during past emergencies, but we were brand new at running the whole show. We had to figure out how to dress under our herringbone coveralls so we wouldn't be too cold out in the corral or too hot next to a Holstein's warm mass. We had to remember the hidden loafing spots down in the lower pasture, and the sinkholes in the corral that would land a person waist deep in a slurry of manure and mud. We had to learn how to turn a delicate pirouette with Lynn's crooked wheelbarrow on the wooden ramp to the dump pile, and how to step lightly through a stanchion for an extra scoop of grain without clanging our heads on the curved metal pipe. We had to adjust to the small changes that threatened the routine of every ordinary day.

The preliminary scrubbing of the bulk tank became a concentrated meditation. Each black rubber gasket along the milk line required a special touch to seal. When everything was clean and connected, the first sucking noise of the vacuum pump started the cows ambling up from the frozen fields toward the barn, and began our race to get finished. One of us swung open the wooden door to let in eight anxious cows from the knee-deep corral; the other snapped the stanchions closed around their necks and delivered eight scoops of grain into the well-licked wooden trough at their heads. Then each of us squeezed in between two steaming cow bodies, rubbing their moist, shorthaired hides before squatting down into the forest of spindly legs. The wash was done carefully, each rough teat stroked clean of the evening's grime with a warm soapy rag until we could feel a bag's fullness. Four stainless steel milking units, their rubber inflations dangling like spiders, were whisked off the hanging nails and onto the first four waiting cows.

There was a pause then; it took a few minutes to milk each cow out. While Tom checked the flow to the bulk tank, I would move to the Dutch doors at the end of the parlor and stare out at the dawn, vaguely aware of the constant high whine of the vacuum line. A slight rise in pitch was my cue to return to work. Gauging the slackness of a cow's bag by feel, I pulled the suckers off one by one, each bringing with it the satisfying *pop* of a soda bottle jerked from pliant lips. Still squatting, I changed the unit over to the next cow, plugging each inflation onto another nipple with a softer *pfloooop*.

Lynn milked twenty-eight big Holsteins and two little Guernseys. Within a couple of weeks, Tom and I knew their names and their idiosyncrasies. We learned to keep a proper distance from the spooky ones and stay on top of the balky milkers. We separated the calves by age and temperament and figured out how to bottle-train the slow learners. We carefully turned down the cuffs of our coveralls after Wednesday's morning milking, so that when Lynn's mother drove up the hill to tackle the week's washing of workclothes, clumps of hay and manure wouldn't clog the washing machine. The arrival of the Darigold truck every other afternoon became an anticipated event, and we kept thinking we were about to fall into a regular pattern of work accomplished and problems solved.

"Yea . . . ahh," Lynn would drawl from the kitchen as we straggled into his mudroom to remove our gear. "I believe you boys are finally getting the hang of those ladies out there."

Except that Tom and I were always tired, and late, and in a bind of one sort or another. Parts along the vacuum line fouled up. The grain bin was always running low. The corrals were so deep in sludge that a slight thaw threatened to swallow the entire herd. It seemed like we spent all our time between milkings chasing cows and fixing fences, so that we fell ever farther behind on the small repairs that kept the system functioning smoothly.

In our growing stupor, Lynn's kitchen held up as our only source of comfort. By the time we finished morning chores and wound our way in past the remains of a family breakfast, an unshaven Lynn, perched atop his red rubber donut, would be curled around his fourth cup of morning coffee. Donna and the three kids would be long gone, and Lynn offered us whatever they had left behind—soggy French toast, brightly colored cereal, boiled coffee. Then he reassured us that his operation had been a success, that the terrible itching was a good sign, that he'd be back in service before we knew it. He met our frequent mistakes and miscalculations with friendly teasing, then offered simple pointers that smoothed our way.

Without dwelling on the inadequacy of our water system, he suggested that we set up a wooden pallet under a showerhead in his basement so we could rinse off after chores. When one old Holstein kept kicking at our hands, he told us where to hit her. A Guernsey heifer freshened and had problems passing her placenta, so Lynn hobbled out to the barn with his syringe and tetracycline. He eased us through our first case of mastitis and a couple of hard births, but any situation beyond our meager knowledge took hours to straighten out.

"It'll be all right," Lynn assured us whenever he caught a hint of discouragement. Then he would deal a second round of chocolate marshmallow pinwheels and tell us another story about growing up in eastern Montana, where the wind had been his only friend. One of his winter chores was sawing ice blocks from a frozen lake to pack between layers of straw so his mother could keep cream fresh during the hot summers. And if we thought his French toast was bad, we should have been with his dad one night when he got caught in a blizzard. He finally stumbled into the shack of an Assiniboine man who offered him supper from a cast-iron pot that hung above the fire.

"Dig deep," the Assiniboine growled as Lynn's dad reached for a second helping. "Puppy on bottom."

After three weeks, Tom and I were crawling from our place to Lynn's in a mumbled blur. We found ourselves eating five meals a day and napping whenever we sat down for an instant. As soon as each milking session was completed, I would lean on the Dutch door and rub Bag Balm into my chapped hands, staring dumbly at a world of black and white and gray. Magpies dotted the snowy fields, while ravens and Clark's nutcrackers swooped down noisily from the cliffs on Purple Flat Top. Naked deciduous trees edging the pastures accented the cold, hard green of the surrounding forest. At night, after the pump was off, the cooing hoots of a pygmy owl bubbled in from the woods. A succession of warm fronts kept a coat of silver fog hanging over everything.

One night near the end of January, the temperature dropped ten degrees while we were milking. As we walked home, the stars shone crystal clear. When Tom and I arrived shivering the next morning, Lynn met us at the door in his fleece-lined Air Force flight jacket and quilted Santa Claus long johns to relay the latest weather report: ten below, and still dropping.

It was frigid in the barn, and after milking, Tom and I strained to remove our bulky clothes in the farmhouse entry-way. Failing several times to get a grip on the zipper of his coveralls, Tom cursed his numb fingers while Lynn chuckled from a chair in the steamy kitchen. When the bumbling got worse, Lynn rose slowly from his donut, came into the mud-room, and carefully ran Tom's zipper down from neck to waist.

"Perk up, boys. Just be glad that wind's not blowing." He moved back to the kitchen to put on a fresh pot of coffee.

"I guess it was February of '58, one morning that ther-mometer started going down and didn't stop till it hit thirty below. The Highway Patrol staked out the road up to Sherman Pass and turned everybody around. Said they didn't want anybody freezing to death in a ditch up there. The next morning it must have been forty below. I put on every coat I had and wrapped up in Donna's big wool scarf. When I switched the pump on, it sounded like the whole system was gonna freeze right there."

Lynn paused so that we could imagine the terror of a para-lyzed milk line.

"I turned the radio up full blast and snuggled close to the cows to keep warm, then had a hell of a time getting them back outside. By the time the sun came up, all I had left to do was feed. When I got up in the barn to get the hay, I noticed Donna's four peacocks sitting on one of the crossbeams."

Lynn darted his wrinkled brow back and forth between Tom and me, imitating the blank stare of the peacocks.

"Something wasn't quite right with those birds. I clapped my hands, but they didn't budge an inch."

Lynn maintained his dramatic stare as he set a box of Corn Flakes on the orange juice pitcher, then plucked a handy yardstick from behind the door.

"So I picked up a long plank and snaked it out along the very edge of that top row of hay. The snot was freezing up my nose, but I eased my board out real slow, thinking they would see the thing coming and jump. I kept pushing until it barely nudged the first bird."

He poked the Corn Flakes with his yardstick. The cereal box tumbled off the pitcher, cleared a syrup-filled plate, and thumped onto the floor.

"*Kerplunk!* Never opened its wings. When I looked down over the bales, that bird was laying feet up on the hay. I touched the rest of the line: one, two, three. Plunk, plunk, plunk. Frozen solid."

Tom and I sat in a trance, mesmerized by the heat of the kitchen and Lynn's waggling yardstick. But Donna had been standing in the doorway for several moments; she bobbed her head up and down as the peacocks hit the hay.

"Huh. You're so full of baloney it's a wonder your donut holds you up. Next you'll be telling 'em about the time Uncle Marvin . . ."

Lynn brightened immediately, brandishing his yardstick at Donna to keep her from stealing the story.

"Son of a gun," he said. "Eastern Montana. That was really a cold night! Uncle Marvin decided he'd better build a fire out in the barnyard to keep his cows from freezing. But the wind carried the flames over into his coal heap, and then he really had a bonfire going. Roasted half his herd. Uncle Marvin said he'd never heard such a cracklin' and a poppin' on the prairie since he visited that Basque sheepherder who kept a stack of dead lambs outside his wagon. Said he liked the way the grease in their wool made his wood stove glow red . . . ."

"Good God, Lynn, there's kids around," Donna huffed, herding the children through the kitchen. We could hear her chortling as the door slammed, and Lynn laughed with her.

"That Uncle Marvin was something else. He ended up running sheep down there in Australia, you know. Saw some terrible things . . . ."

Tom and I milked for many days in a row. Each evening after the vacuum pump was finally turned off, I leaned out those Dutch doors to listen. The pygmy owl faded away into the winter nights, and occasional great horned owl hoots began to boom in from the hillside to the north. It stayed cold and clear for more than a week before a quiet storm brought almost a foot of snow, and the cows marched into the parlor drenched and stinking. Gradually the big flakes turned into a slow, sloppy rain.

From the direction of a birch grove down in the alfalfa field, the persistent grating whistles of a saw-whet owl began to pierce the mist. The whistles continued through several drizzly days, and I realized that the saw-whet must be setting up its breeding territory—time was moving toward spring. Lynn's four weeks were up, with a couple to spare, and we still hadn't heard any news of our retirement. He seemed more cheerful of late and was getting around better, but whenever I saw him grimace as he stepped onto his icy porch, I had to wonder how soon he could deal with a schedule of deep squats in the milking parlor. And when a simple foray to town took him all day, I had to wonder how soon he wanted to return.

One afternoon, Lynn slogged out to the milking parlor as Tom and I ground through the chores. He had just come back from a doctor's appointment in Spokane and was obviously keyed up.

"You fellas really missed something," he said, tugging at the brim of his white go-to-town cowboy hat. "Just as I was coming out of the doctor's office, three fire engines went screaming past. I followed 'em down the block to that old building with the jewelry store on the bottom and funny brickwork on the top. You should've seen the flames. About all the firemen could do was try to save the stores around it."

Tom and I shuffled around the cows, keeping our dull routine. We were both aware that this was Lynn's first unsolicited appearance in the barn since his operation.

"I couldn't stop staring at those burning walls," Lynn continued. "It was like I was hypnotized. A fire escape tore loose and came crashing down into the street—I almost couldn't move out of the way. All I could think about was Pusan."

Lynn had often spoken about his experiences in Korea—he had joined the Air Force as a teenager and was aboard a troopship on the way across the Pacific when the armistice was declared. He continued on to Korea to be stationed in Pusan as part of the American deployment. But I didn't recall hearing about a fire.

"We were piecing the railroad back together, you know. During the day we'd go out and work on the tracks. At night we slept in our tents on a hill above town. The war was just over, and refugees from all over the country were pouring into Pusan."

The whine of the vacuum line rose in frequency, and I knelt to switch a unit.

"Late one night we heard all this screaming and yelling. I jumped out of my tent, and it was as bright as day. The refugee camp was on fire, people running away like ants from a hill. We just stood there and watched the whole place burn—*whoof!* It was all cardboard shacks, packed right together. A couple of hours later, there wasn't much left of Pusan."

Just as I completed my changeover, the new cow swung up an artful kick that sent hoses and steel clattering across the slick floor. Lynn slipped in on the other side of the cow, replaced the unit in a practiced flash, and stood up talking.

"We spent the next three days down there helping clean it all up. Took every piece of equipment we had. Everywhere you looked there were people pushing wagons and carts, on the way to bury their dead."

Except for the sucking noise of the milking units, the parlor remained quiet. Beyond my cow's back legs, I watched the toe of Lynn's cowboy boot grind a cigarette butt into the concrete floor. Then Tom slapped his hands together to shoo the last bunch of the evening into the darkness of the barn-yard. Starting to life, I stepped across the feedway to get at the hay. Lynn, released from the spell he had cast, moved along with me.

"Anyway," he said, "somebody on the sidewalk was telling me there was a safe in the basement of that jewelry store, filled with diamonds and rubies and who knows what. I'm thinking about driving back in tomorrow morning to watch 'em dig it out."

It was the first week in March now, and winter's end had reached its soggiest point. The continuous veil of fog seemed to bleed the green out of the landscape, so that some days we couldn't see the tops of the trees. People walked the streets with their heads down, sidestepping puddles. Mud was every-where, freezing into a splattered crust at night, covered by violent snow squalls during the day, oozing into kitchens and living rooms. Tom was anxious to get started on a remodel project downtown, but we couldn't think of setting a founda-tion until the frost left the ground.

That was the way things stood as I leaned out the barn door for another evening's rumination. We had finished milking, but there was no satisfaction in it—just that morning we had lost our second calf to scours, and the Darigold truck had been so late for its pickup that we overflowed the bulk tank and made a horrible mess. The woods around our place still held fifteen inches of snow, and the sputtering thaw dashed any hopes of a walkable crust. I knew that with each step on the way home my boots would sink in over their tops. Craning my head around the outside of the door, I squinted at a thermometer on the barn wall: fifty degrees. It was the first time the mercury had touched that mark since mid-November.

A mournful noise sounded somewhere nearby. A dog, I thought. A coyote. Almost a goose. Another yapping moan, like a baby, made me look up. More primordial barks drifted down across the fields.

Nothing happened for a few moments. Then the day's last glimmers of sunlight glanced off something high above, exactly as alpenglow strikes a mountain peak after darkness has settled below. The round body of a bird moved slowly across the sky, one tiny point of reflected light against the backdrop of dusk. The bright spot advanced steadily, emitting more faint barks, until it disappeared among the tangle of treetops to the north. I tipped my head back to let the sounds enter my ears and stared into the first spring evening of the year.

Tom came running from the calf pen, his hair standing straight up. "Swans, right?" he shouted. "Must be!"

I nodded, and he strode into the dark, declaring, "I think we just made it through the winter."

After another week of warm breezes, the valley floor began to dry out. Inspired by the swan migration and a quick bloom of buttercups behind the snow, I talked my way into a natural history column for the local newspaper. By the end of March, Lynn was back milking full-time, grousing about the business but handling it all with ease. Tom and I stayed busy right through the summer; we ran into Lynn once in a while downtown but kept away from his farm during milking hours.

I was out for a walk one September evening when I heard the dull murmur of machinery in the oat field adjoining our land. In the growing darkness one big headlight glared off Lynn's ancient red combine. With its balloon tires and complaining roar, the thing looked like a B-17 bomber taxiing into position for takeoff. Lynn hunched forward off his seat, using body English and violent gestures to keep all of the sprockets clanking. Catching sight of me in the dusk, he waved wildly and clamped down on his brakes. When I waded through the fresh oat stalks to climb up beside him, he slapped me heartily on the back and lurched ahead into the grain.

"Sold 'em!" he hollered, looking straight ahead at the falling oats. "By God, we sold 'em today!"

I thought he must be referring to his grain harvest, then realized that at this hour of the day he should in the barn milking. At my quizzical glance he burst into laughter.

"They went down the road this afternoon—every cow on the place. Some fool up on Blue Creek thinks he wants to go into the dairy business. Me, I don't care if I never see another milk cow again."

Lynn wrenched the combine around a tight corner in the field. "Yep," he said, "we're gonna try the beef business for a while."

FOURTH OF JULY

MIDMORNING SUN CRACKLED HEAT through the tin roof of the crusher house, a single large room propped up on stout tamarack stilts at the edge of the old Finch Quarry. A thick layer of grayish brown rock dust coated the silent machinery inside. As I walked toward the window for a breath of fresh air, I noticed a small bird's nest tucked into the lower left corner of the sill. Within the bundle of twigs sat a soft gray ball with a washed yellow breast and a faint crest on the back of its head. The bird eyed my movements closely but did not stir a feather. I inched forward until I could see the stiff, insect-funneling bristles arranged around its bill. A western flycatcher.

All the glass panes in the window were broken, so that the bird could have flown at any time. "Go on now," I whispered to it, hoping Kenny might not hear. "Time to get away."

Kenny Wuesthoff looked up from the cast-iron flywheel in front of him. His face was flushed with exertion, and his scalp glowed red beneath his crewcut. The eight-foot arc of the flywheel rose above his head like a gigantic ship's wheel. The graceful spokes radiating out from its hub contrasted with his square, powerful hands, which at the moment were patting a lump of plastic explosive into the angle where one spoke met the bottom rim of the flywheel. Beyond his fingertips, I could read the date 1908 stamped into the heavy cast iron.

"Ken," I said. "You sure you want to do this? I'll be happy to bang on it some more with the sledge."

"Ohhhh no," he answered. "I've had enough of beating on this mother. She's going to feel the big hammer now." Turning back to the window, I cupped my fingers together and slowly closed in on the flycatcher, until it jumped up with a squeak and escaped through an empty pane. In its nest I counted four opal-white eggs, each splattered with rusty spots on one end. The flycatcher circled back, then landed lightly in the low branch of an alder tree just outside the window. Twitching its tail, it grated out a steady barrage of alarm notes. Beyond its tree, the abandoned diggings of the Finch crawled up a steep slope of the Huckleberry Range.

This quarry had once held a large, clean deposit of magnesite, a mineral not often found in commercial quantities. Valued for its stability at high temperatures, magnesite was formed into bricks that lined every blast furnace in Pittsburgh at the turn of the century. Austria reigned as the world's main supplier of the mineral until she lined up with the Central Powers for World War I. Then geologists urgently focused on the Huckleberry deposits west of Chewelah, and the Finch Quarry provided the original raw material for the Northwest Magnesite Company.

The flywheel that Kenny was preparing to demolish had been anchored in the crusher house since the quarry's beginning. Its job was to turn the belt that opened and closed the jaws of the primary crusher, which set the refining process in motion by smashing large rocks into smaller ones. At first its revolutions were powered by the long, slow strokes of a steam engine. My friend Wynn Cook remembered it that way, from the end of World War I. He was a boy of fourteen then, managing a team of workhorses that pulled wagons full of rock from the quarry to the crusher. According to Wynn, the new Model T flatbeds could not stand up to the rough floor of the quarry, whereas a few clucks of the tongue kept his big farm horses plodding back and forth all day long.

The flywheel turned steadily above the weight of Wynn Cook's wagonloads. It turned as the ore was pounded and floated, then transferred into the ore cars of a legendary cable tramway that stretched five miles downhill to the main reduction plant on the edge of town. It turned as new quarries unzipped the green Huckleberry forests, adding names like Double Eagle, Red Marble, and Keystone to the local lore, and didn't halt until the Depression forced the company to shut down production in 1937. Many of the laid-off workers found jobs in the flurry of construction at Grand Coulee Dam until the flywheel, powered by an electric motor this time, started turning again a year later. It whirred steadily through World War II, when the plant shipped out five hundred tons of concentrate a day. It spun on as the crusher chewed rocks for a new processing line that mixed ground magnesite with cottonwood shavings to make panels of Thermax insulation board.

The flywheel was still revolving in the early 1950s when a winter storm blew in and dropped two feet of snow at the quarry. Another twelve inches fell the next day, then six more overnight. Two men working up at the Finch had to stop the flywheel's turning while they waited for some Samaritan to break through the drifts. Several of the county snowplows got very stuck trying, then the best motor grader from the valley plant bogged down halfway up the hill. The marooned workers sat in the crusher room for three days before someone managed to get a sandwich to them.

By then, Chewelah had evolved into a company town. "The Magnesite," as the company was locally known, meant summer jobs for high school kids and top-notch recreation equipment in the park. Company supervisors provided a steady pool of Boy Scout troop leaders. Struggling farmers made their land payments by working the swing shift and shoveled free fertilizer from the fine dust of the spill pile. While some townspeople worried about the sterile grainfields downwind from the plant and the incidence of emphysema among the Thermax workers, most accepted the Magnesite because it provided a steady, predictable pulse to the economy of the whole community.

Then in the early 1960s, a Dallas-based company acquired controlling interest in Northwest Magnesite and began to take account of changes in markets and technology. On March 1, 1968, the new owners announced they were shutting down the plant and laying off all the workers. Within a breathtakingly short time, the ore cars that had zinged along the tramway for half a century hung motionless in the air. The dump trucks at the Finch poured their last loads of blasted rock onto the battered screen over the crusher. The ancient flywheel made one last revolution and eased noiselessly to a halt.

🐦

Kenny drummed his fingers on the stippled rim of the idle flywheel. "You step outside and around the corner," he said, as he pulled a length of fuse from his shirt pocket. "I'll be along in a minute."

I moved toward the door of the small building, avoiding several lengths of angle iron and a heavy I-beam that we had cut loose earlier with Kenny's acetylene torch. Once outside I circled around to the alder tree on the chance that I might be able to shoo the flycatcher farther away from the window and its nest. The bird was nowhere in sight. I slid down a tailings pile toward a thicker line of trees and dropped into a gravel sink that offered good protection from three sides. Waiting in my foxhole for Kenny to set his fuse, I tried to retrace the chain of events that had landed me in this particular spot on a sunny Fourth of July.

The links stretched back to the first summer Tom and I spent in Chewelah, only two years after the Magnesite's closure. On our way into town, we passed beneath the ruins of the huge plant. Within a week, we had peered into all the stores on Main Street, some of them recently boarded up. One establishment still open for business was the Oasis Tavern, which served big hamburgers and lip-blistering jo-jo potatoes to go along with their draft Rainier. A regular group of men was always gathered around a table by the front window, playing pinochle, laughing and jawing. On our third or fourth visit we noticed a new face at the table, a fast-talking young fellow in the middle of a tale about how his friend Merle had incited a Bigfoot frenzy the previous winter by fashioning a set of five-toed snowshoes and setting off across the countryside after a good snowstorm.

When the guy saw that Tom and I were laughing, he strutted over and introduced himself as Kenny Wuesthoff. He bought us one round, then another, and with a quick wit began to challenge every move either of us made. It wasn't too long before he and Tom were locked in an arm wrestling match on the bar. When Tom managed to put him down, Kenny shrugged it off without missing a beat.

"Doesn't bother me," he said, then recounted an auto accident down in Texas that he miraculously survived. He pulled up one leg of his black Ben Davis work pants to reveal a logging boot padded with a three-inch heel. "I've been sawed off before and managed to grow back."

It was a couple of summers later that Kenny lost his license, for driving under the influence. In need of work, I signed on to serve as his chauffeur and assistant. Kenny's avocation at that time was salvaging parts of the former Magnesite operation. It was my first experience in the scrap business, and I found it exhilarating to watch somebody single-handedly dismantle an empire. His headquarters was a gravel pit crammed with the essentials for taking things apart. Business deals were conducted in messy backyards and dark cocktail lounges, in a language I often didn't understand. Early on, Kenny showed me where to find the price of scrap metal in the newspaper and made me figure out the ratio of time versus weight to make sure I was earning my wages. I learned how to cut steel with an acetylene torch and how to shatter old cast iron with a hammer. He always encouraged me to hit things one extra time, because the foundry operator he sold to in Yakima liked his scrap in small chunks with no impurities: "Number One Prepared."

Kenny would tackle anything. After I had helped him take apart a few minor buildings and tanks, he finagled the salvage rights to the aerial tramway that had connected the Finch with the processing plant near town. At an Army surplus sale he found a Studebaker Rio two-ton truck crane with six-wheel drive for navigating rough terrain. Demonstrating considerable dexterity at the controls of the Rio, he rigged a crazy-looking reel contraption onto the boom. With this setup we took to the hills, slurping up miles of steel cable from the tramline like strands of well-oiled spaghetti. When all the wire rope was gone, we snipped the angle-iron towers apart like Tinkertoys and shipped them off, too, until nothing was left of all the invention and engineering that had gone into the tramway except thousands of slag-covered bolts scattered about in the pine grass. For days we walked the hillsides beneath the missing towers, stooping down with greedy fingers to pick up the steel bolts. "Hi-grade," Kenny called them, and figured we were pulling in about sixty dollars an hour.

Not even the Fourth of July holiday could slow him down; after we cleaned up the tramline, he immediately won a bid to dismantle the old Finch crusher house and all contents therein. Today was our first day on the job.

"*All clear?*" Kenny shouted from the window of the crusher house.

I stood up in my foxhole to look once more for the unfortunate flycatcher, but all I could see was the shadow of its nest in the empty window frame.

"Ready," I called back.

"Well, we got *fire in the hole*," Kenny yelled. "They're gonna hear these fireworks clear down at the parade." His heavy black boots clomped down the wooden stairs of the building and away through the serviceberry.

As I ducked behind my barrier, sheltering my ears against an explosion, I thought about Chewelah's Fourth of July parade from the year before. After the passage of some crepe-paper floats and a candy-throwing clown in a Model T pickup, a platoon of logging trucks had rumbled by. The last one pulled a trailer containing the butt log of a mammoth yellow pine. I followed that log all the way through town, and after the truck pulled over in the city park, I climbed up to count 365 annual rings. The driver knew exactly where the tree came from: "The old Keystone quarry, you bet. The Magnesite people left some beautiful timber up there." He described a series of elevated islands sticking up twenty and thirty feet off the quarry floor, created as the diggers followed veins of ore around the quarry. Atop these mounds grew a few enormous yellow pines and Douglas fir. "I don't know how anybody's ever gonna get to 'em, but it sure seems a shame to let 'em go." The logger climbed up on the truck with me and pointed to a pattern of punky wood that ran across the rings like a bolt of fat lightning. "See that rot? I think we got to this old soldier just in time."

A sharp flat *ka-whap* broke through my ears. It broke again, through layers much deeper down, and I looked up to see the shape of a bird catapulted clear of the open window in a burst of uncontrolled flight. The shape disappeared as shrapnel from the heavy flywheel whistled overhead, and I hit the dirt. Heavy thuds shook the serviceberry uphill. A gentle shower of smaller particles, splinters and steel, rained down upon the slope. I waited until the patter ceased before lifting my head again.

Ears ringing, I walked up the tailings slope and past the alder to meet Kenny. From outside, the building looked exactly the same as it had before the blast. We tiptoed back up the steps and peered through the doorway at pieces of fly-wheel dispersed about the floor like halibut on a lucky fisherman's deck.

"Number One *Pre*-pared," pronounced Kenny as he uncoiled the hose of the acetylene torch. "Why don't you carry what you can out to the truck. I'll cut away a couple more of these struts here so we can get to that conveyor next."

Before I started lugging, I went to look at the window. The corner where the nest had been was swept clean. I leaned out the opening to search the alder branches and rough slope. Nothing. Behind me, I heard an exclamatory hiss from Kenny's torch, then the thud of something heavy hitting the floor.

"Got me!" he barked.

I turned around to see him wobble across the room, the torch still blazing in one hand while he pressed the other tight against his forehead. A thin stream of blood seeped between his fingers and dripped onto a hunk of the blasted flywheel, bright red against the duns of cast iron and dust.

Kenny pointed the torch at a sharp edge of angle iron that had grazed him on its way down. He pressed hard on his forehead, trying to scotch the flow of blood, and handed me the torch. I closed off the flame, then pried his fingers off the gash.

"Stitches," I told him, stuffing a handkerchief between his fingers and the cut. "Don't think there's any way around it."

Kenny sat down on a chunk of the flywheel. He didn't appear to be in shock. "Any fool knows you don't work past lunch on a holiday," he said. "Let's get these tools loaded."

He stood up, flicked the hanky out of his eyes, and grabbed the sledgehammer one-handed on his way out. I retrieved the torch and followed close behind in case he lost his bearings; only when I crossed the threshold did I notice that the door had been blown clean off its hinges. As we padded down the stairs, a western flycatcher sallied across in front of us. It nipped for an insect, then swooped to its perch on the alder branch opposite the empty window.

THE LORD'S WORK

CAROLINA BECK WAS NOT THE KIND of person you would expect to cut up in church, so I didn't know what to think when she began to chuckle right out loud in the middle of the service. She had invited me to her Wednesday night prayer meeting, and even though we arrived a little late, she marched me straight down the center aisle to the front pew, where she obviously was accustomed to sitting.

As a fuzzy-cheeked pastor a fraction her age sermonized directly above us, Granny Beck nudged me with a sharp elbow, whipped her white wool scarf across the bottom of her face, and hissed "horseradish." I realized that she was mimicking me and how ridiculous I had looked standing in her kitchen earlier that afternoon with a dish towel tied over my nose, trying to fend off the daggers of fresh horseradish that shot from her meat grinder. I smiled along with her, but the mirth suddenly passed from her eyes, as if she had taken a bite of something terribly bitter.

"Dis is de way I choost to do it," she said, in a German accent that clipped all the soft consonants and seemed to make whispering impossible. Blue veins stood out on her hands as she tightened her grip on the scarf. "But no matter how close I hold it, I still taste de grit."

I had known Granny Beck long enough to appreciate the quick leaps her mind could take and guessed that she was thinking about the dryland wheat country. The feel of the scarf across her face must have reminded her of the dust storms that used to scour her farm.

She reset her ramrod back against the pew, giving the pastor her rapt attention for a moment. He had begun his message with a passage from St. John's Book of Revelation detailing the unsettled days that would mark the end of our civilization. To suggest that those final days might be drawing nigh, he had brought in a stack of newspapers and was reading aloud accounts of relentless civil war, massive displacement and emigration, and a spaceship that had crash-landed in a remote part of Mongolia.

Carrie clucked at each new disaster, then turned to me. "Not so different from what my own people suffered through, you know. And that was just the beginning for them."

Her grandparents were native Germans; during a time of political upheaval, they relocated to Siberia, which hadn't suited her father at all. When he was nineteen he walked all the way across Russia to avoid the draft, and from the Black Sea hopped a tramp steamer that eventually landed him in the United States. He found a wife among German-Russian immigrants in North Dakota and married her in 1886. They started their family of seven there in Dakota—Carrie came along in 1894—and finished it in the wheat country of eastern Washington, near a settlement called Ruff. A passing photographer took a picture of all nine of them lined up in front of their tiny house, with nothing but sagebrush scablands in the background. When they mailed the photo to family left in Siberia, the relatives wrote back, outraged: How could you have prospered so much in the New World and not remembered to share some of your wealth with us?

"That sagebrush," Carrie once told me. "It was everywhere." To clear the land, her father got a piece of railroad steel and hooked a draft horse to each end. As they dragged the rail across the hillsides, uprooted sage rolled out behind the bar. "It was us kids' job to stack up the bushes—they was the only thing we had to burn. We'd pile them as high as we could and then climb to the top and jump them down so the wind couldn't blow them away. Oooh, how we reeked of the desert."

Around the same time that Carrie's parents met in the Dakotas, a boy named Gustof Beck was born to a German couple teaching modern farming techniques to peasants in Odessa, Russia. Little Gustof's father died, and his mother remarried and left the boy to live with an uncle. Soon after he came of age, soldiers arrived to conscript him into the army. It was nighttime, and Gust, who was supposedly sleeping in his uncle's barn, was nowhere to be found. One officer finally grabbed a pitchfork and began to stab haystacks over and over. Gust was burrowed inside the hay, all right, flinching this way and that to escape the thrusting tines. Neither threats nor cold steel could flush him out.

As soon as he was old enough, Gust worked his way across Europe, then stowed away on a boat bound for North America. He caught up with his mother in Ruff, where he found a job running a threshing machine during wheat harvest. Within the year he had married his boss's teenaged daughter, Carolina.

Gust and Carrie's first home lay down in the coulees of the Columbia's Big Bend, and for a while things worked out fine. Gust's mother came to live with them, and Carrie gave birth to five children. Their people had always been Congregationalists, but in the 1920s a certain Elder Riffle came into the community with an alluring message. He dunked Carrie and Gust in the Columbia River, baptizing them as Seventh Day Adventists. Since then, Carrie had faithfully observed the Sabbath between sundown Friday and sundown Saturday.

"Oh, I might wiggle sometime," she liked to say. "But mostly I try to sit."

Not long after the time of the Becks' conversion, the dry years of the Dust Bowl enveloped the region. Carrie developed a compulsion about dust, sweeping constantly, draping rags over dishes and foodstuffs, shedding tears as wind-driven soil crept across the threshold and piled up on windowsills. For seven years—seven straight years—between 1925 and 1931, the drought winds blew Gust's wheat seed out of the ground. In that year the Becks finally gave up and took their five kids, two horses, one milk cow, and fifty dollars north to the Colville Valley.

"You should have seen my kids when we first come into those pine trees below Spokane. Oh they was nervous. They kept asking 'When will we be out of the trees, Mother?' I told them we was never again going to be out of the trees."

The Becks rented a farm and hired out as dairy hands, gradually building up their own herd on the strength of the entire family's effort. Then in the 1940s, one of her boys went away to the war, and Carrie's stomach started to bother her. Her daughters told her she was fretting too much. "I got my reasons to worry," she answered. She endured bleeding ulcers until she was seriously anemic; in 1943, two operations removed over half of her stomach, and liver shots were the only thing keeping her hemoglobin on the chart. One evening a couple of years later, Gust went to gather the cows for evening milking and didn't return. They found him down in the pasture, unconscious, and soon afterward he was diagnosed with stomach cancer and a bad heart. They were forced to quit the farm and move into town, where Gust drove a dump truck for a local miner. That was the beginning of the time of cures.

Carrie often recalled how resourceful they had been on the farm. "We always ate everything, didn't waste nothing of the whole pig from snout to tail. That was before some good people woke me up and told me about nutrition." She journeyed to Canada to learn about a new diet program, and although she never could get Gust to give up barn-cured sausage and headcheese, he didn't mind when she began selling bulk food out of their house—early Loma Linda-brand soybean products that came in cans and tasted like the art on the labels.

Then, sometime in the 1950s, Carrie had an experience with an angel. A light glowed at the foot of her bed, and a smile filled the entire room. Without undergoing any drastic transformation—"It seemed like the most natural thing in the world for it to be standing there"—Carrie suddenly felt herself possessed with the strength to take control of her own healing. She made herself well, then better than well. Her health food business, a tittering joke to some people, swelled into a going concern. When Gust's heart finally burst, instead of faltering she expanded: along with the church's Dorcas Society she rented a small house downtown and began selling her wares.

I first walked through the door in 1970, attracted by the smell of fresh-baked bread. Granny Beck, then in her late seventies, sat behind a steel cash box and several fifty-pound grain sacks that she husked about whenever she felt they needed rearranging. There were other elderly women in the room, talking lightly as they snipped rags. A teenager holding a small child was squeezed against the wall reading labels on the vitamin shelf. Granny Beck was a natural saleswoman, and I staggered out under the weight of bagged almonds, a sack of buckwheat flour, bunches of dirty beets, more carob powder than I could consume in the next decade, several cans of soy things, and two petite chicken pillows that the Dorcas ladies had stitched up for a church drive. I soon learned that people from all over the area came into that small room for handouts, medical advice, and spiritual comfort as well as food. "Dr. Beck," some of them called her.

"Chooo, that 'Doctor,'" Carrie laughed. "They don't get no doctor when they come to me."

She laughed like that now, a sneezing exclamation that marked the end of the Wednesday service, and the pastor happily dismissed us all. Several of her children and neighbors offered us a lift, but Granny Beck waved them off, then set out with the same fervor that had allowed her ancestors to conquer the Ural Mountains and hoof across Europe. Manly glasses glinting in the moonlight, shoulders squared, she swung her wagon-spoke arms and grasped the air.

"Get your hands out of your pockets!" she admonished me. "Breathe!"

As we goose-stepped along her circuitous walking route, Carrie kept her face focused sternly ahead. Her sun-worn visage, small in proportion to her broad shoulders, hinted at something wild trying to go domestic. She swept down the quiet town streets and across a footbridge over Chewelah Creek, pausing only when we reached the tower housing the Cushing Eells Memorial Bell. By then my arms had gone a little numb from so much slinging.

The bell tower stands near the spot where the missionary Cushing Eells and his companion Elkanah Walker held the first Christian service in the valley, at the camp of an Indian they called The Fool. Granny Beck, looking around as if some stragglers from that 1838 event might still be loitering about, turned to me with an expression of concern.

"This man was a Catholic, was he?" she asked.

"Congregationalist," I answered.

"Ahh," she said. "My people. Before we all crossed over to the Adventists, I mean. I've known many good Congregationalist brothers in my time. Many fine preachers, too."

I had to tell her that I didn't think the Reverends Eells and Walker had won too many converts at their first service. The natives were more impressed with the number of blankets the white men slept under than with their sermons on the Second Coming, and the missionaries complained that their interpreter could find no word in the Spokane language to match the Christian concept of atonement.

"That's all right," said Carrie, reaching out to pat the blue steel struts of the bell tower. "As long as they was doing the Lord's work."

She started walking again, headed now toward a much-desired supper. That afternoon, while I was digging horseradish from the edges of her garden and tearfully grinding it into pulp, she had cooked up an unlikely mixture of food. There were her famous cheese pockets, pastry dough filled with rennetless white cheese; bounty from her garden chopped into the makings of chow mein, waiting only for a can of crunchy Chun King noodles; a generous bowl of the autumn's first sauerkraut, spooned from one of the procession of stone crocks that simmered pungently in her sitting room. She hadn't quite had time to whip up a dessert, and as we covered the last block of the walk home, something sweet was on her mind.

"I could make steurm, you know, those little fried dough balls? Ach, they is so bad, but it's all right to jump over the fence once in a while."

She passed by the steps of her front porch to take one more look at her garden. It was October, the beginning of a dark, cold time in the Colville Valley, but her plot was still producing. Kale and mustard greens stood up smartly against her church shoes. She patted a basketball-sized Savoy cabbage to feel if it might be ready for her crocks. Locating by memory and touch, she jerked up some white daikon radishes in a shower of rich loam.

"How cold, do you suppose?" she asked, watching the white puffs of our breath gather into fog above her plants. "I think we're hard enough to take a frost, but maybe not the pumpkins." She started forward and then stopped, cocking her head like a bird. "But what's this?"

Beside the garden was a wooden garage that sheltered her retired '57 Plymouth. The structure was sided with scalloped asbestos shingles that had once been painted mint green. In the glow of the street light, we could see bright splashes of new color against that faded green; below them lay what appeared to be jumbled heads, like a vision from Sleepy Hollow. Carrie stood small and confused, completely taken aback. Apparently some mischief makers had bounced her pumpkin crop against the shed. After a few moments, she hiked up her church dress and began climbing among the vines, but it was useless. The pumpkins were all shattered.

"So beautiful," she sighed. "Why, do you think?"

Pawing through the wreckage at the base of the garage, I tried to come up with something to say. It occurred to me that it was football season, and that the team did walk right past her house on the way home from practice every evening. Carrie came over beside me and picked up a fragment of a ribbed shell. While she held it there, steady, I could see the vinegar come back into her work-toughened hand.

"Blachinda—pumpkin tarts!" She sniffed the piece of pumpkin in her hand and nodded. "Yah. I got strudel dough in the freezer, and the pressure cooker is still out. I can have them in the oven before we finish our chow mein. Just help me pick up what we can use here, and we'll leave the rest for tomorrow."

We felt our way around in the grass, grasping for the slimy orange strings of pumpkin flesh. Only once did Granny Beck grumble, "Oh! Those boys!" When her hands were full, she clutched the pieces to her chest and made her way toward the kitchen door.

CAROUSEL

I SLOWED FOR THE SECOND HALF OF THE big switchback on the way down the hill, taking in the scene at the Chewelah town dump as I drifted past. Two fresh dump-truck loads of used bricks dwarfed the other trash heaps. Even though it was early, a brown Pontiac sedan was already backed up between the piles, its trunk open. A lone man sat on a milk crate in front of the rubble, patiently whacking old mortar off a brick with a mason's trowel. As he rocked forward, his bald head shone like burnished leather.

I had seen him around town a time or two—a large man, always alone, with luminous skin and a thoughtful face. I wondered exactly how old he might be—past retirement, certainly, but I couldn't tell whether by years or decades. He wore striped bib overalls, farmer style, but he didn't move like a farmer. Seated on the crate, his weight balanced over his knees, the man looked more like a musician ready to play.

He was still there when I came back up the hill in the late afternoon and turned into the dump for a look around. I walked past the trunk of the Pontiac, counting eight neat rows of bricks laid inside it, and stopped alongside the man in the overalls as a burst of gray mortar sprang away from his trowel.

"Hello," I ventured.

He looked up, then reached into the breast pocket of his bibs to touch the control button on a hearing aid.

"Second load of the day," he said, pointing his trowel at the sagging rear of the Pontiac. His words came out in short, smooth bursts that varied oddly in volume. "I've about had enough. Good bricks though. Look at this."

He plucked one from the pile beside his milk crate and handed it to me. Stamped into the clay was the imprint of the Chewelah Brick Company.

"They used to have a fellow down there named Ehorn who knew his business. I'm Shirley LaMont. Who are you?"

I introduced myself and we shook hands. Shirley's seemed soft and expressive for a man who had just spent all day cleaning bricks. He withdrew his hand and, with a nod that discouraged further conversation, bent back to his work. I took one turn around the dump, listening to the pleasant whangs of his trowel, and left for home.

A couple of months later I stopped by the newspaper office to drop off my weekly column and was greeted by utter chaos. The Chewelah Independent was leaping into the computer age and had hired Kenny Wuesthoff to get their old equipment out of the way. He had transported the linotype machine intact to the local museum, but the ancient printing press was too wide to get out of the building; at the moment of my entry, Kenny was trimming gears and cogs off one side of the beast with his sledgehammer.

I knew this change was in the works and had asked Kenny to save the old layout table that graced the top of the press. It consisted of two sections of heavy wood hinged together, each wide enough to display a pair of open newspapers side by side. Although the surfaces were black with printer's ink, I thought a few sessions with a belt sander might turn the table into a serviceable desk. Now, to protect my interest, I slipped between the secretaries and back to the scene of Kenny's relentless banging.

"Just in time," he said as the tabletop I was after crashed onto the floor. "Help me get this thing out of here."

Together we maneuvered the heavy slab out the double doors into the alley. As we leaned it against the outside wall, Shirley LaMont stepped out from behind Kenny's flatbed truck.

"Holy Cow!" shouted Kenny. "It's Jesse James. Should we load this thing right in your car, Mr. James, or would you like it *dee*-livered?"

Shirley did not reply immediately but continued to inspect the battered hunks of cast iron that were headed for the foundry. As before, he wore striped bib overalls over a long-sleeved khaki shirt, and moved with a slow grace.

"Did you have to break it up so bad?" he asked.

"Get my hammer over here, pronto," Kenny directed me. "Mr. James needs this load busted down into smaller pieces."

Shirley chuckled at that, even as he moved on to inspect the odds and ends Kenny had flung into the alley. He stooped to touch a pair of smooth lead ingots once destined to be melted into letters for the linotype machine, and shuffled in a figure eight as he consolidated several hardened lead splatters into a pile beside the ingots. Then a series of forged wrenches, each shaped to deal with a different part of the press, caught his attention.

"Go easy there, Jesse," said Kenny, as he towed a heavy section of the printing press out the doors. "The wrenches are mine."

Shirley abandoned the tools to gather up some silvered metallic printing plates that warbled at his touch. Drawing a pair of reading glasses from his bibs, he perused a couple of metal pages silently, then let out a grunt of surprise and walked toward us, reading an advertisement.

COME OUT
of the
KITCHEN
These Hot Days
EAT at the
MANHATTAN
Something good
Every Day
MANHATTAN CAFE

C. E. LaMont

"That was my dad's place," Shirley said. "I think he and Mom wrote this up themselves."

He laid the silvered sheet over by itself and continued his survey. When he reached my layout table, he bent close and ran his fingertips along the inky surface. Motioning me over, he pointed to a line of graffiti scratched on the bottom— "THE CHICAGO KID 1927."

"Hmmmm," Shirley said. "I wonder who that might have been." He straightened and rapped the table smartly with his knuckles. "I believe you'll find this is made out of nicely joined sugar maple planks, all quarter-sawn. You should take good care of it."

Kenny stepped to the door to fling another armload of scrap toward his flatbed, and Shirley caught his eye like an experienced bidder capturing the attention of an auctioneer, pointing at the printing plate with the ad for his parents' restaurant and at a short stack of glass photo plates I hadn't even noticed. Kenny nodded his OK, adding, "I knew you were going to rob us sooner or later. Anything else we can do for you?"

"That will be enough for now, thank you," Shirley replied.

He methodically wrapped the glass plates in newspaper and loaded them into the trunk of his Pontiac. The ad sheet received special attention in the back seat, where it sang again as he smoothed it against the upholstery. Satisfied with his arrangement, Shirley climbed in and drove away. Kenny, an unusually contemplative look on his face, turned to me.

"I've known a lot of people who like to pick up scrap, but Mr. LaMont there has what I'd call a broader interest."

Over the next several years, Shirley LaMont lingered around the periphery of my doings, and our brief encounters only whetted my curiosity. Once, on my way home, I spotted him sifting through junk at the town dump; when I stopped, he greeted me cordially and explained the market value of a hand-cranked coffee grinder he had just raked out of a pile. Another day, I happened to glance out the window of the hardware store just in time to see him present a little girl with a perfectly folded square newspaper cap. Shirley adjusted the hat on the child's head, then sauntered into the post office, wearing an identical paper cap of his own. At the Valley Fair one August, he appeared as the croupier of a penny-toss game. Sporting a green eyeshade and a butcher's apron, he ramrodded the action around a sheet of plywood painted with a neat grid of red and blue numbers.

"There's a man for adventure," he called out when he saw me. "Come on over here and take a chance."

Every now and then, when an opportunity presented itself, I would ask people around town what they knew about Shirley. One local merchant told me that Shirley came from an island in the Caribbean, where he had held some kind of position in society. That was bunk, a nurse at the hospital countered—if he was so rich, why was he washing the hospital's linens in a laundry behind his house? Her husband took issue: "Come on, all Shirley ever did at his place was cut keys. Well, maybe he did sharpen a few lawn-mower blades on that contraption he had that looked like a hay baler. But only a few. And how could the man run a laundromat when he was never home? All the summers I can remember he was rambling around the countryside with that ding-dong merry-go-round of his."

A merry-go-round?

"That's right. Hauled it on a flatbed truck from here clear across the Colville Reservation. The guy was never at home."

At the Oasis, I encountered a woman who once worked as a waitress in the Manhattan Cafe. It was just before the Depression, she said, and Shirley's dad was the cook. Shirley was a young man then and would come in sometimes on Saturday night to play banjo or ukulele for the crowd. My friend Walt, who overheard her story, told me that as a kid he used to hang around the Manhattan during those sessions. He would wait for Shirley to take a break so that he could sneak up to the bandstand and finger a few chords on the banjo.

Late one winter Tom and I landed a job remodeling a house just up the street from Shirley's place. On a March morning during a period of freeze-thaw-freeze that had left the ground all crunchy and heaved up, I found myself stretched out underneath the reclamation project, trying to jack up a sagging girder. The house was an old one, supported by stone pillars here and there. Beyond the warped timber, my visible world consisted of a one-foot strip of daylight along the bottom of the walls. I had taken the first couple of pumps on my hydraulic jack when slow, grinding footsteps announced a visitor to the job site.

Twisting my head a few inches, I saw a rubber-tipped cane probing the edge of my under-house world. Behind it two brown Hush Puppies gingerly stepped across crushed ice crystals. Thick white wool socks billowed around their tops. The shoelaces were untied, and above them flapped a vertical pattern of hickory-striped pants. The Hush Puppies stopped, and I could hear heavy breathing above. Then Shirley's voice spilled out, lustrously projected like a big band singer spitting out a novelty song.

"What d'you know? Black-backed three-toed woodpeckers have three toes. They show up on recent burns to feast on the fresh larvae of bark beetles. Anyone who knows last summer's Rainbow Lake fire can have another go at it by walking up there this spring and watching the woodpeckers work to and fro on all the beetles that have moved into the burned trees. You can note all your regular favorites— sapsucker, flicker, hairy, downy, pileated—and some funny ones besides. So! Don't forget to count those toes."

Shirley began to laugh then, a deep rumble that grew as it moved up from his belly. He had me all right, pinned under the house while he pinwheeled the words from my latest newspaper article into a ditty. I wriggled my way out from the crawl space to share the joke; Shirley waggled his head and rapped his walking stick against the side of the house as he repeated, "Don't forget to count those toes!" Then he took three steps, leaned on his cane, and picked up a bent nail. A few more steps and he nabbed two rusted spikes that I had pulled from a rotting skirt board. It had been a long skirt board, and Shirley swatted at a whole line of twisted nails with his stick, corralling them into a pile.

"Such waste," he said. "Don't know if I want to have a fellow that doesn't bother picking up his nails to work for me or not. Some of these are hardly even bent."

I couldn't miss the fact that Shirley was breathing hard from his effort. His voice wheezed, and his lips, usually full and expressive, had faded to thin liver.

"Listen," he said, "I've got a little job over at my house that needs finishing. Just a matter of a few bricks on a hearth. Half a day's work, I'd say. Come over and see me after you get done on this place."

I had to tell Shirley that I was going to be tied up right here for two or three months.

"That's all right," he said. "I'll keep track of you. I suppose we'll have enough time."

Shirley was as good as his word, visiting several days a week to offer suggestions. He thought the studs we were using looked awful warped. The drain field was a joke—how could liquid leach from a pipe that lay below the water table six months of the year? And certainly he had never seen anybody cast aside so many good nails. "Careless, careless," he grumbled.

Sometimes I would be on the verge of getting upset with him, but he would back off, have a hearty laugh at my expense, and pull a section of some outdated newspaper from his back pocket. Then we would talk about things that led us far away from the job site—the gold mine over in Republic, say, or how to properly stew a rabbit—but never, when I thought back on it, anything very personal. I really wanted to ask Shirley about that carousel he was rumored to have, but there was something about his manner—a reticence that hinted at deep reserves—that kept me from ever bringing it up.

As the framing of the remodel job closed in, Shirley's social visits became less frequent. I hadn't seen him in several weeks when I called him about the job he wanted finished.

"Come in the morning, but not too early," he said. "Bring your trowels and some mortar mix. I believe I have enough bricks to see us through."

I waited until almost ten to make my appearance. Shirley's home was a modest farmhouse that he had modernized with brick courses up to the bottom of the windows. The job wasn't entirely completed; a sheet of plywood slanted upward where the front steps belonged. Beside it lay a dozen or so sash weights from outdated double-hung windows that looked a lot like weights Tom and I had removed from the house up the street.

I walked around to the side yard, where a series of outbuildings and lean-tos sprawled out behind the garage. The complex was roofed with a crazy quilt of multicolored tin, and my eyes fell on a vintage ore cart filled with rusting automobile starters and alternators. Beyond the cart a walkway led into a maze of used bricks and sawmill slabs stacked waist-high. I was edging back for a closer look when Shirley's wife, Doris, tiny and quiet, cleared her throat from the side door of the house. I jumped to attention.

"He's inside," she said, holding the door for me. Shirley was parked in an easy chair in the living room, the tube from an oxygen tank taped beneath his nostrils. He had lost weight, and his flesh sagged. It took some effort for him to reply when I asked him how he was doing.

"Not worth a damn," he said. "My stomach feels like a peeled onion, and my feet are swelling up like balloons. They want me to check into the hospital for a bunch of tests, but I know once I go in there, it's going to be awful hard to get out."

He paused to catch his breath, closing his eyes and inhaling shallowly through his nose. Sprinkled around the room were recent family photos of children and grandchildren, gathered from around the country. Shirley's rubber-tipped cane rested against the wall near his chair, and a black leather-bound daybook sat within reach on a small table.

He opened his eyes and lifted his head. "But that's enough of that. Right there's what we need to talk about," he pointed behind me to a small fireplace in the corner. The simple firebox was surrounded by cut terrazzo triangles that splayed outward in a stunning sunburst—rays of ivory and smoke, fawn and ochre, rose and purple, all polished to show their distinctive chips of local marble. I rubbed my palm along the smooth surface and tight mortar joints in admiration.

"I did that," Shirley said. "But I never had the time to finish the base for it. I want you to lay those last few bricks along the hearth. You can just set those boxes there off to the side and get started."

The hearth was practically hidden beneath an array of cardboard boxes. As I began moving them out of the way, I saw that the first one was completely full of postcards, topped by a tinted photo of the *Idaho Queen* ferry plying the St. Joe River.

"Nice card," I said.

"Yes it is," agreed Shirley, momentarily perking up. "Might be from my parents' honeymoon. Clarence and Nellie. You know how busy they were around then? My mother married Clarence in Coeur d'Alene in nineteen and nine, gave birth to me in Terre Haute, Indiana, in nineteen and ten, and managed to have my brother, Delmar, in Spokane in nineteen and eleven. My dad cooked, you know, and bounced around. What did we count once, twenty-seven different restaurants?"

Shirley sank deeper into his chair, and any interest in his wandering parents seemed to drift away. As I returned the *Idaho Queen* to the box, I noticed that the card beneath it showed another vessel, "The World's Largest Auto Ferry," groaning under the weight of three steam locomotives. I thought I'd ask Shirley about that one, too.

"Yes, yes," he said, waving me off. "My folks took me on that in 1917 when my dad was cooking in Yerington, Nevada, during the war. That was the way you visited San Francisco in those days. Of course I remember it. I was already in school then. Look, there are hundreds of cards in that box. Maybe you can come back some other time and sightsee, when we aren't paying you good money."

I shut the box flaps over the postcards and picked up the next carton, which was stuffed full of what looked like pocket diaries. "I didn't know you wrote," I said.

"I don't," he answered. "I'm not that much of a fool."

His voice was gruff. Hurriedly I snatched the next box off the hearth and swung it over to one side. With a thump, the bottom fell out, and suddenly the floor was littered with photographs of all sizes and descriptions. A distinct stutter of laughter crept into Shirley's long sigh, and I took my time picking up the pictures.

One grainy snapshot captured a banjo-wielding Shirley beside an accordion player in the Legion Hall. Shirley looked sharp in pressed pants, dark shirt, and checked necktie. He was seated with perfect posture on a bench; his partner was a little more slumped, and they both looked like they were enjoying themselves.

There were several notices for band dances, most of them around Chewelah. Shirley was always seated off to the right, holding his banjo in playing position. One color print included horns and a big bass drum. The face of the drum was painted with a carefully rendered tropical scene of waving palm trees. I walked it over to Shirley's chair so he could see it, too.

"Yeah, I painted that drum," he admitted. "It was for Marge Rathdrum's fiftieth birthday party, and I was the one who kept a bass drum around to thump. If I was by myself, I would sit down and use the foot pedal, but I never liked it.

Always looking for somebody else to play the thing. What I
liked was to be part of the band."

The next picture had been snapped much earlier, when
Shirley still had hair. He and a friend knelt with guitars in
front of a partially blocked sign on a clapboard building.
Shirley had no trouble recognizing the fancy letters.

"That's the Manhattan Cafe in downtown Chewelah,
right around 1930, one year after I got married. The Manhattan was a pretty decent place, and that fellow and I would
play there in the evening sometimes while my dad cooked.
There's a picture of him somewhere in this mess with his
chef's hat on.

"I never thought I'd stay in this town for the rest of my
life, but I guess I moved so much as a kid that by the time we
got to Chewelah I didn't want to go anywhere anymore. Tried
working at a sawmill, but the sawdust got to me. Did a stint
at the county garage. Spent one season at the Magnesite,
making insulation board, but my lungs couldn't hack it.
That's when I decided I could make it on my wits, and I
haven't worked for anybody since. She didn't always think
much of the idea, though."

He pointed to a stray picture of a large handsome woman
with Shirley's look about her. His mother wore a white
muslin dress that touched the bare ground and a broad-
brimmed black hat with a ribbon that hung to her waist.
Although a mining-camp shack and open desert loomed in
the background, the two boys were decked out in freshly
pressed white short pants and long-sleeved shirts. Shirley had
on black leggings and button-up shoes. At age seven he was
whippet-thin, and his dark eyes penetrated the camera. His
brother, Delmar, younger and still pudgy, held the family cat.

"I don't know how she did it," Shirley said, "but Mother
always kept us dressed in the best of clothes." He held the
photo at arm's length and studied their outfits.

"This was taken the year before the meningitis got Delmar. And right after was when I broke my arm. The doctor wrapped it all up, and then the day I got the cast off, I broke it again." He shook his head in dismay.

"Look, I'm tired. Are you here to talk or lay brick?"

Shirley napped in the chair while I laid the bricks across his hearth. The oxygen tube remained taped to his nose, taking an awkward turn when his head slumped onto his right shoulder. Doris busied herself in the kitchen but came in to check on him every once in a while. I worked slowly, studying the terrazzo pattern in front of me. The newspapers that formed my dropcloth came from Terre Haute, Republic, and Yerington. They all carried dates from the current year.

The Roman bricks cut square, and I finished up just as Doris nudged Shirley awake for lunch. Somehow his sleep had made him look even worse, and I tried to gather up my tools with as little fuss as possible. Shirley leaned forward in the chair to pick up his cane and used it to count off each brick on the hearth. There was no hiding the fact that the grainy Roman bricks were a poor match for his smooth terrazzo sunburst. He wrinkled his nose around the oxygen tube in a show of dissatisfaction.

"That's the way I figured it, though," he said. "So I guess it'll have to do." He jerked his head toward the kitchen. "Tell her to write you out a check for twenty-five dollars. And while she's doing it, here." Shirley reached laboriously into his bibs for a ring of keys and dangled it in front of me.

"I saw you out there nosing around before you came in. Take these keys and have yourself a good look. Everything's still wired in, so don't hit any switches."

He closed his eyes, and I retreated via the side steps. The third key I tried unlocked the garage, and I stepped inside to a dizzying collision of sights and smells. There were soaped horse collars on the wall and Skookum blocks still rigged with fresh hemp rope. One whole wall was lined with rows of Prestone antifreeze cans, secured together and tipped sideways to form shelves that were crammed full of rusty hardware.

There was indeed a laundry, all set up and well used; around the machines a faint scent of singed cotton still hung in the air. An extractor with a beaten copper drum had the brand name ARROW laid into its lid in open filigree. On top of a mangler sat the hand-cranked coffee grinder, still smelling of grounds, that Shirley had rescued from the dump. Tucked behind the door was the square plywood coin-toss game that I had played at the Valley Fair. Clear letters printed down all four edges of the square board read COINS MUST CLEAR LINE.

I left the garage and wound back to the next shed. When I clicked the padlock open and stepped inside, it was like walking into the clutches of a giant mechanical spider—arms and wires all folded up and draped back on themselves. Around the perimeter of the frame ran a wavy decorated canvas, delicate next to the power train of automobile under-parts. The horses were handmade and identical in shape, differentiated only by their paint jobs: Appaloosa, white, dappled gray. Tattered paper patterns for their different parts were tacked onto one wall. Each animal consisted of a body jigsawed from thick planed lumber, with a shoulder and haunch joined to it by two bolts, and a head that nodded from the neck. The final touches consisted of two ears and a tail, plus a painted mouth turned up in a smile. When the carousel was set up the horses must have hung from above and twirled around in smooth circles like the little planes I had ridden in at other county fairs. Suspended from a nail on a rafter I found a roll of twenty-five-cent tickets, and beside them a scrap of paper on which Shirley had penciled an itin-erary of his circuit in the summer of 1951.

July 28–Aug 1	Curlew
Aug 2–3–4	Republic
6–9	Omak
11–13	Brewster
15–19	Pateros
21–24	Mock
25–28	Oroville
30–31	Cusick
Sept 2	Addy
4–6	Valley

Shirley was still asleep when I slipped back into the living room. Doris handed me my check and asked if it was right. She said she was afraid they were going to have to go to the hospital that week and take those tests. I said I hoped they turned out well and began to gather up the last of my tools.

"Wait a minute," Shirley groaned from his chair. His voice was weak, and he didn't make any effort to lift his head from the cushion. "Did you find everything you need out there? Got me all figured out?"

"Shirley," I said. "I don't even have a clue."

"Good. Go home and get yourself some lunch."

I stuffed the key ring into his breast pocket and whisk-broomed the mortar joints on the hearth one more time. Shirley raised his right hand for a wave.

"Maybe you could come back later this summer and finish those steps out front. We're getting mighty tired of that piece of plywood laying up there."

"Any time, Shirley," I said, and slipped out the door.

SPORTIN' LIFE

*D*ARRELL SOMERSET LEANED INTO
the guitar, his round face breaking into a profuse
sweat. His fingers didn't exactly fly along the fret
board—you could see them searching, sometimes uncertainly,
for the next chord of the country swing solo he was chasing
down. But his pick hand was strong and touched off notes
with the kind of vigor that created music. It made me smile.
It made Darrell's wife, Eileen, rattle a mason jar she was holding against her thigh. It made Mike Reynolds, cleaning up the
bones of the fingerling trout she had fried for our supper, bob
her head at the kitchen sink. It made Mike's husband, Babe,
an older, silver-haired fox never easy to please, stick his face
down next to the sound hole of the guitar while he kept time
with his forefinger. Beads of sweat broke loose to roll down
Darrell's cheek, and as he circled from the bridge to the last
verse, he double-timed the one-string melody right through to

the end. Then he breathed, apparently for the first time since he started, and handed the vintage Martin back to Babe.

"Happy Halloween to you, sir," Darrell said, pleased with his performance.

"Was that 'Glow Little Glow Worm'?" asked Babe, accepting his Martin and lightly strumming the hot strings with his silky touch.

"We always called it the 'Guitar Boogie,'" answered Darrell, taking a swig from his stubby Rainier. He laughed heartily, and his boyish face warmed another degree. "But 'Glow You Glow Worm' is fine by me. You're the boss here."

Babe was indeed the boss of his spread along Chewelah Creek, and now he was set to demonstrate that he was the master of his instrument as well. He fingered a diminished chord on the Martin, walked effortlessly down the neck, and with a purple crooning of the line "Riding through a canyon . . .," glided into "The Cowboy's Lullaby." It was Zane Grey crossed with Tony Bennett, and everyone in the room had to sit tight and admire the smoothness of the show. I sneaked in one more fish before Babe wound up the tune with a flourish, leaving Darrell to shake his head in open amazement.

"Man," he said. "When you get your fingers going against each other like that, it's way past me. How do you keep track of where you are?"

Babe gave a hearty stage laugh and leaned forward again. "You know what?" he whispered loudly. "I can hear those changes coming from a mile away."

Babe had a keen sense of how to meld the elements of a song into a smooth finished product, a craftsman's intuition that extended into his daily work. He was a blacksmith by trade, and the first time I saw him, in the spotless shop behind his house, he was waiting for a heated shovel blade to fade from wheat straw to cherry red so that he could quench it for a perfect temper. Babe's neat complex of buildings lay just across the creek from Purple Flat Top, and he became the natural person for Tom and me to turn to for advice on anything mechanical. When we acquired a small sawmill that had been lying in pieces behind someone's barn for three decades, Babe knew exactly how to set it up, on precision steel so it would saw boards straight and true. When we needed a fancy brass and steel door latch, it was Babe who pulled out a length of silver brazing rod and joined the two materials with a delicate, continuous bead. He was a magician with pulleys and blocks; on one job Tom and I hired him to rig a high line for hoisting trusses, then enjoyed a day of free-flying fun as we floated them into position on the house frame.

"Zero tolerance" was one of Babe's favorite sayings, often uttered just before he lost patience with me for being slow to pick up his directions. I figured that was my shortcoming, and my loss; I would often leave Babe and Tom dueling with their tape measures in the shop and walk up to the cabin for a talk with Mike. She was a diligent worker, too, but she operated more on instinct and enthusiasm. Her wildflower rock gardens attracted a host of songbirds, and our sightings often ended up in my newspaper column, accompanied by one of Mike's pen and ink sketches.

Responding to a gesture from Babe, Mike left her dishes in the sink to join him as he strummed a lead-in to a tricky locomotive number. Her little-girl speaking voice suddenly dropped in pitch and rose in volume as she hit every mark Babe laid out. They laughed their way through three tempo changes and a tough hill climb and still finished the train ride exactly together, like an act in a well-rehearsed show.

PURPLE FLAT TOP

I clapped along with the Somersets, and Mike blushed to the roots of her platinum hairdo.

"Well, shoot," she giggled. "Fifty years of practice should be enough to get one song down right."

I knew that Babe and Mike had gotten married when they were still in their teens and had waded through some hard times before retiring in Chewelah. Eileen and Darrell hadn't been together nearly that long—this was a second marriage for both—but they seemed a natural fit. Darrell was born in Oklahoma, then moved with his dad to Colorado and New Mexico before striking out on his own. He followed construction jobs up the spine of the Rockies and was working as a journeyman in Pasco when he met Eileen. She had grown up in the rangeland of eastern Oregon, and when a line contracting company offered Darrell a job in Stevens County, she was happy to settle down in a place with some trees.

Babe sold the Somersets twenty acres of land, and over the summer months Tom and I made periodic visits to monitor their house-building progress. Their site lay right beside Chewelah Creek, and we were amazed when Darrell simply dug a channel back from a fishing hole, sank some concrete casings, dropped in a pump, and started plumbing. It wasn't long before the Somersets created the feel of a burgeoning homestead alongside the creek.

Eileen was due to have a baby before Christmas, and while Babe took a break from playing, the conversation turned to the new couple's preparations for the upcoming winter. The trees that Darrell had cleared for his yard would provide their firewood, even if most of it was green enough to make Babe wince—they had a tight stove, Darrell pointed out, and once you got the stuff started, it burned all right. He figured all he needed was a few dry tamaracks to use as banking wood and he'd be set. They had their meat—he'd shot his deer right above the house, then bagged a cow elk down in the Blue Mountains. And work was going pretty good—it was all set jobs, running the new installations into houses or repairing storm damage during emergencies. Darrell liked to climb poles.

"Sometimes it's confusing though," he said. "You get one of those danged poles on the ground, and you know you have to have this much on this side, and maybe you need a cross-bar this way to catch another line coming across, and then they decide they want one more lead going off that way. You bolt 'em together down on the ground and look at it, and then you got to imagine what it's going to look like up in the air."

Babe snorted, as he did when anybody was about to make an obvious mistake. He stood up, announced that he was going outside to take a leak, and begged the ladies to excuse him. Darrell ignored the interruption and kept talking.

"I did one yesterday afternoon, last thing, and had it all spiked up and ready to raise. Our foreman came around and said 'Hold on a minute now, Darrell. Maybe we'd better wait till Monday on this baby.' I looked at it again, and every strut was ninety degrees off."

Eileen got a kick out of that, and the jar she had been carrying all evening rattled in her hand again.

"What's that you have there, honey?" Mike asked, and Eileen smiled, obviously glad that someone had finally noticed. Her fingers, swollen from hard work and pregnancy, slowly unscrewed the lid and poured the jar's contents on Mike's kitchen table.

"What in the world are those?" fluttered Mike.

"Beans," Eileen answered. "Remember Uncle Mack, when he was around this summer? He sent us these for seed. Said if he couldn't make it up next spring, we might have to get the garden going on our own."

Everybody remembered Uncle Mack. He had arrived at the beginning of summer, planted a lush garden, and stuck around until the freezer held enough vegetables to balance Darrell's venison. In his late seventies, Mack was a stoop-shouldered man with a round face and the look of a South-western Indian about him. His home was Chalma, New Mexico, at around eight thousand feet. There he had a sawmill for cutting the "quaking," his term for aspen. Tom and I liked the way Mack made it sound and looked around until we found some fire-killed aspen. The logs were light, the bark a chalky white. The one-inch boards fell off the blade like butter, free of sap and practically scentless, with irregular brown knots that winked like cat's eyes.

Babe came back in and strolled past us into the bedroom. He emerged with a second guitar and held up its slate black body for all to see.

"This is my Washburn," he announced. "She's an old-timer, like me. When I was eighteen years old a guy paid me a hundred dollars to dress up like a Mexican troubadour and croon with this baby under a lady's window all night long. Had bangles hanging all the way around my sombrero." Babe shook his head, just remembering how sharp he had looked. "And I earned my money, too. Back then I could go from sundown to sunup and never repeat the same song."

Babe stuck the Washburn in Darrell's arms, took up the Martin himself, and proposed a duet. While they tuned up, Mike and I examined Uncle Mack's beans. They were larger than pintos and flattened almost like limas. Some were white with rich buckskin figuring, others pink with darker blotches, and a few seemed to be roasted to a delicious scarlet. No matter what the background color, a clear, clean pattern stood out on each bean.

"Uncle Mack found them in a cave in the mountains," Eileen explained. "Up in the Pueblo country. He was crawl-ing around when he found a bunch of pots lined up along the walls, and some of the pots had beans in them. Mack said at

first he meant to leave everything alone, but then he decided
that it couldn't hurt to take one little handful home."

Timing his entrance, Babe broke in:

> Green beans, soya beans,
> Black beans, and turtle beans.
> Well I'm not too keen on those beans
> Unless they are the
> Chili chili chili beans.

He cued Darrell to jump directly back to the song's beginning but shut it down when Darrell didn't quite make the
leap. Babe scowled a mild version of his scowl and turned so
that Darrell could look squarely at his hands on the instrument. "Watch me," he said. "And try listening, too."

The two returned to their strumming, and Eileen to her
beans. "He planted them in his garden—Uncle Mack was
always a gardener—and they taste so good you won't believe
it. He's been growing them ever since and gives some away to
people he likes. Calls them his magic Pueblo beans."

Eileen counted out two dozen for me, all colors, and
another twenty-four for Mike. In my hand they looked like
river rocks, worn smooth and shiny by time.

"Now!" Babe shouted at Darrell. "Now! There's the seventh right there! Can't you hear it coming around? Good
god, man, it's right under your nose."

Darrell shook his head. He squeezed the neck of the
Washburn for a minute, then held out the guitar to its right-
ful owner.

"You'd better take this, Babe. I don't think I'm the one
that's supposed to play it. But thanks for supper, and thanks
for letting me try."

Eileen quickly swept the rest of Uncle Mack's beans back
into her jar, and she and Darrell moved for the door. I stood
up, too, bumping my knee hard against the kitchen bar.

"Yeah," I said. "I didn't know it was so late."

The Somersets said good night quickly; Mike was still squeaking out a protest as the door shut behind them.

"Well for goodness sake," she appealed to me. "Don't they know not to take Babe seriously? Shame on you, Babo."

Babe ignored her. With his left hand he placed his Martin carefully on the sofa, then caressed the old black Washburn. Situating himself like a soldier in a kitchen chair, eyes straight ahead, he ran all the way through "Java Jive" without missing a lick.

"Say," he said upon finishing. "What happened to Darrell? I was hoping he'd stick around and play some tunes with me."

It was some time before I heard another tune from Darrell Somerset. Eileen had her baby, a chubby boy they named Darrell Lee Junior. I went over to their cabin to google over him once, but missed Darrell, who was working out of town. The next year Eileen became pregnant again, had some kind of complication, and lost the baby. When I saw her downtown after that, her complexion was ashy white. Little Darrell Junior, spiffy in new cowboy boots and an oversized black hat, looked round and good-humored like his dad. Eileen wanted to know if I was still keeping up with those beans and laughed when I told her I had raised just enough to keep for seed.

Tom got married about that time, and I started my own house farther down the bench. I didn't get across the creek as often as I once had, but one evening I did find my way over to the Reynolds's, where Mike was sputtering with the news that Darrell had run off to Pasco with another woman. When I paid a sympathy call to Eileen shortly afterward, she seemed like a strong woman determined to keep her place going and take care of her growing boy. Each time Darrell's name came up, she punctuated it with a jagged laugh.

A year or so after that Tom and I drove to Springdale on a Saturday night to listen to some music at the Crown Tavern. The band there featured Joe Abrahamson, a familiar figure from the Spokane Reservation who could warble out the country and western tunes. The crowd was sparse when we arrived, and the band rambled through their first few numbers as if having a conversation among themselves. Joe wore a huge black cowboy hat pulled down over his eyes, so that when he sang out "Hey, Good Lookin'," all you could see was his crooked grin.

By ten thirty, however, business was brisker. During an instrumental version of "Sleepwalk" Joe worked his way around the tables to greet the crowd. He was out of sight in a far corner when a small ruckus erupted around him. Then I saw him break clear, dragging another man by the arm.

"And now, ladies and gentlemen," he crowed from the stage, "My friend here is going to honor us with a song. It's Darrell Somerset!"

Darrell stood with the band, sporting the same boyish grin and floppy gray cowboy hat that I remembered. He wore boots, blue jeans, and one of those rodeo belt buckles that can cradle an ample stomach. But what took me completely by surprise was the way he gathered himself together and faced the microphone. He surveyed the audience, nodding here and there to acquaintances, then turned back to the band and said crisply, "Ready boys?"

The instruments broke out at twice their earlier volume, curling through a tight recapitulation of the last four bars of a Hank Thompson standard. Darrell drew his hands up before the mike and addressed it in a voice full of mischief and starch. The buzz from the tables quieted immediately, and the audience followed a story they had heard a hundred times.

I didn't know God made honky tonk angels
And I should have known you would never make
    a wife.
You gave up the only man who ever loved you
And went back to the wild side of life.

Darrell sang it like a blues, as if he were in Kansas City
instead of Springdale. He cocked his head and bent notes of
wonderful pain. His face broke out in an honest sweat, and he
whipped off his hat to wipe his brow with a forearm. During
the guitar break he and Joe stomped their boots together in a
snappy line dance, and then Joe took the high harmony
behind Darrell's final moaning chorus. When they finished to
whoops and banging beer glasses, Joe grabbed Darrell's fist
like a boxing referee and thrust it over his head.

"How about it, ladies and gentlemen?" he yelled. "Darrell
Somerset!"

It took a minute for the noise level to resume its regular
Saturday night hum, and for Joe to take off on another subdued set of familiar tunes. Halfway through the second song,
Darrell appeared in front of our table, looking like his regular
shy self.

"Hiya fellas," he said. "Mind if I join you for a minute?"

Tom pulled out an extra chair, and we congratulated
Darrell on his sterling performance. He said he was living in
Ephrata and working for another electrical outfit, driving all
over the Columbia Basin to climb poles and string line. It
turned out he had met Joe Abrahamson in a bar over in the
Okanogan Valley some years before; since then they got
together whenever they had the chance. And the singing?

"Shoot," said Darrell. "There's nothing to that. I've
always liked to sing. But I still can't play the guitar worth a
hoot. Say, how is Babe, anyway? Still sore at the world?"

Babe, of course, hadn't changed a bit, but with the mention of his name the image of Darrell's place by the creek filtered into the room, smelling of green pine. The three of us fell into an awkward silence. I scraped most of the label off my beer bottle while Darrell composed himself, fitting silent words together. Tom studied the pattern of rings beneath his glass and finally stood up.

"Ready?"

I stood up, too. "Guess we might as well head home."

"Glad I ran into you," Darrell said, and his expression showed he meant it. "Don't see anybody from up the creek much anymore."

He shook our hands and relaxed back into his chair. With an open palm he tapped out the finish to the Merle Haggard tune that Joe was singing.

"Ready?" Tom asked again, and we turned to leave.

"That's the way it is sometimes," Darrell called after us. "When you gotta go, you just gotta go."

EAGLE MINE

ONE OF THE LAST OF SPRING'S HEAVY, wet snowfalls caught me down at the Chewelah Grange, perusing the seed rack as people sloshed their way in and out of the unwelcome mess. I looked up from the peas in time to see a fairly new Dodge pickup pull up beside the gas pumps and Sam Baker emerge from the cab. His black rubber boots dripped white with a peculiar gummy clay, and his black work pants shared smears of the same color. His shiny pickup, new Pendleton shirt, and snappy suspenders indicated that something must be brewing in the Baker household. I hadn't seen Sam for months, but I had heard rumors that he was reopening an old silver mine on Eagle Mountain, just east of town. He caught my eye through the window and walked straight over after pumping his gas.

"Ladder stock!" he said, grinning through the weathered features of his freckled face. His voice was quiet, as always, but carried conviction. His wire-rimmed glasses twisted wildly away from his big ears, and wisps of reddish gray hair crept out beneath his stocking cap. He leaned forward on his feet, comfortable but ready to go.

"You still running that toy sawmill up on the hill?" he persisted. "I need some ladder stock."

Sam didn't tell me why he needed ladders, or what he had found inside the old Eagle Mountain mine; instead, he spent twenty minutes cheerfully complaining about the weather, his crew, the people who had originally sunk the shafts and yellow pine as a structural timber. Yet I knew that silver prices were up, and his high spirits made it seem possible that he was onto something good.

"I'll be up there after lunch," he said, ending his discourse with an invitation. "If you can get some decent boards together, bring them on up and have a look."

Early that afternoon, with a couple dozen rough-cut two-by-fours clattering in the bed of my truck, I turned onto the muddy road up Eagle Mountain and churned past the few houses spread along the lower part of the hill. A right fork led into thick second-growth forest dominated by tall firs and dripping cedars. There was a good deal of snow left at this elevation, and the recent storm had made the road tough to negotiate. Inevitably, my pickup skidded off the beaten track, and I was on my knees stringing tire chains when Sam powered up the road in his four-wheel-drive. We transferred the boards and left my pickup dead in its tracks.

The road grew steeper and narrower, but Sam built up a good head of steam and kept going. He took a minute to tease me about my newspaper column—"your little bullshit stories"—then commented on a recent article about the soil conditions that grow calypso orchids and morel mushrooms.

"Hell," he said, "you should go deeper, tell people what's underneath that dirt. I've been reading geology in this country for years by driving back roads and looking at trees and colors and outcrops. It's true—I can tell what's going on below the ground by looking at what's on top of it, but I try to explain that to people and they think I'm nuts. Course none of them have been looking at rocks as long as I have, either."

Sam was raised in the desert country of eastern Oregon, in a family with the mining bug. A local story had it that at age sixteen he had been pounding on a claim with a pickax when he chopped into a vein of pure sugar gold; in one afternoon he supposedly tapped out several thousand dollars worth of ore and became hooked forever on the trade. Sam prepared himself for the prospecting life by taking a degree in mining engineering at the state university. There he met his wife, Ida, and together they moved back to the east side of the Cascades. With Ida often handling the assay lab work, their territory expanded across the Great Basin and beyond, but Sam almost always had a project of some sort going in Stevens County.

We circled around one last wild switchback and ground to a halt. The portal to his mine was nothing more than a black space gouged into the green hillside, but the area surrounding the timbered entrance presented a scene of quiet desolation that would have comforted Bret Harte. A big rubber-tired air compressor squatted in the middle of a rugged flat area outside the mine's entrance. Dull red high-pressure hoses snaked into the portal, providing workers inside with air power. The compressor's stuttering noise filled the air, so I poked around by myself while Sam rummaged through papers and tools on the dashboard of his truck.

Slender lines of narrow-gauge railway track emerged from the dark portal, zipping across a small level area through stray boards and lengths of air hose. Supported by a pair of fresh timber posts, the rails halted in suspension over the edge of the slope. Directly below, piles of dynamited rock lay in puddles of the same gooey white clay that covered Sam's boots. All the recent dumpings, as well as the scrap lumber, tools, and steel laid out on the site, had been frosted white by the morning snowstorm.

Among several rigs parked around the compressor was the battered Ford pickup that until today had been the only thing I ever saw Sam drive. A human form, clad in greasy coveralls and a yellow miner's hat, pored over a dismantled pump at the truck's tailgate.

"Eskimo," Sam shouted in my ear. "From Little Diomede Island. I spent the summer on the Alaska coast, trying to get gold out of some gravel up there. My whole crew was Eskimo, and I brought this one back with me. He's damn smart; I think I might be able to make a miner out of him."

Sam walked over to his crewman and yelled some indiscernible command. The man looked up, apparently realizing for the first time that we were there. Beneath his splattered hardhat the Inuit wore thick black glasses, which he adjusted with a greasy forefinger as he aimed a string of curses at the malfunctioning pump. Sam encouraged him in his best gruff voice of authority, then moved along to check a gauge on his compressor. He seemed perfectly at home on this frozen scrape, his every move focused and engaged. This was a real mining job, the culmination of countless hours on the hunt, and the excitement that surrounded Sam sparked back through all the generations of prospectors who had pleaded with these hills to yield them wealth.

Independent miners in the Inland Northwest have always been a small and self-reliant group. Most of them prospected for gold, then silver. As the glitter dulled down toward lead and zinc, they scattered to specialized markets that they hoped would support their struggles long enough to get back to gold. Everybody was aware of everyone else's claims and intimately familiar with any ore body that actually made it as a commercial venture; often the same claim changed hands among them several times. The miners freely offered their views on how a particular operation was laid out, how well somebody could manage a crushing plant or a rebellious crew, and why their latest claim was certain to pay off soon.

Tom's father, Fay Bristol, was a player in this world and never missed the Northwest Mining Association's annual convention in Spokane. Our first year in Stevens County, Tom and I drove in to meet him at the Davenport Hotel, itself a monument to the region's first big silver boom. Fay was having a fine time in his room on the eighth floor, and took us into the bathroom to show us the three spigots over the sink—one for hot, one for cold, and one that used to draw ice water up from a barrel in the depths of the building.

"I guess they had some poor fellow down there shoveling ice all day long," Fay marveled. "But they sure didn't need him during the week of the mining convention. All these guys drink their whiskey straight."

When Fay judged it time to join the festivities downstairs, he loaned me a brown linen sport coat that I could have wrapped twice around my torso, borrowed another for Tom from a friend down the hall, and guided us into an elevator that sank toward the elegant Davenport lobby. The gilt doors opened onto a madhouse, wall-to-wall miners come to town for the year's biggest rendezvous. Fay knew every one of them, and Tom and I soon found ourselves on our own. As we were elbowing our way around the edge of the lobby toward a stomping good big band, we suddenly found ourselves face-up to the front paws of an enormous polar bear. At least nine feet tall, the creature had been stuffed and mounted in dead attack position.

Beneath the rangy spread of the bear's forelegs, a trio of miners lamented the host of new regulations that had just been signed into law. Small-timers didn't have a chance anymore, one was saying, and before we knew it the government and large companies were going to take over everything. His companions agreed so vigorously that I was afraid they might topple the polar bear. Tom and I were circling the animal, looking at the tufts of coarse white fur that stuck up on its back like small moths, when Sam Baker materialized out of the crowd. We had met him only once before, one afternoon in town with Fay, but he recognized us and raised his glass amid the chaos to offer us a toast.

"It's water," he confided, lifting his glass again. "I just hold onto this so the bartenders will leave me alone."

He held his ground with a wrestler's grace, smiling. The din of the lobby ruled out any attempt at normal conversation, so the three of us just stood there, bobbing warmly among the continuous waves of people. After a few minutes Sam patted Tom and me on the shoulders of our oversized jackets and told us to come by the house if we ever needed anything.

It was only a few weeks later that we needed some outsized timber washers to cinch together a set of trusses. Sam's offer immediately came to mind, and in good time I found myself climbing onto his front porch. His rambling house was surrounded by big maple trees and an assortment of treasures that spilled over two adjacent lots. Most of the pieces were on the large side—washing machines modified into ore separators, copper-lined sluice boxes, forty-foot I-beams—and I couldn't imagine how I might find something as small as a timber washer among them. But when Sam answered the door, chewing on his lunch, he was sure he knew right where they were.

"Come on in for a minute, though," he offered. "We're almost done."

He sat back down at the table and put the finishing touch on his meal by carefully spreading thick layers of peanut butter and honey on a hunk of homemade bread, then attempting to eat the slithering mass before it dripped onto his wrists. Ida was quietly dismantling a make-believe castle that the youngest of their six kids had draped around the living room. She moved with a smooth, slightly distracted manner, and while Sam turned his hands this way and that, trying to direct the flow of honey, she brought me up to date on a crustacean study that their oldest daughter was conducting in the North Atlantic.

"Now," interrupted Sam, after he finally got the best of his honey ball. "Let's go outside and see if we can get you those washers."

We headed across the yard to the school-bus body that housed his welder. Inside, he pried the lid off a dynamite box crammed full of miscellaneous fasteners and produced a couple dozen large-sized timber washers.

"This what you're looking for?" he asked. "If these don't work, come on back and we'll find something that will."

At the entrance to Eagle Mine, Sam sifted through a steel box for a schematic map that diagrammed sixty years of digging in Eagle Mountain.

"O.K., this is your crosscut tunnel right here, and this is the drift we'll be following." He jabbed at the jumble of expanding, multidirectional lines on the dirty paper, then saw the look of confusion on my face. "Never mind, we'll get back to that later," he said, and launched into a quick history of mining in the immediate vicinity. In 1910 United Copper opened a large operation on a mountain straight across from Eagle; nearly every commercial building still standing in

Chewelah was constructed during the next few years. Silver, copper, lead, and zinc were extracted all over the county for the next two decades, and the industry ran strong until mineral prices crashed during the Depression.

Some of the best strikes from the early boom were consolidated around Eagle Mountain. Sam had learned about the specific geology of this hill in the mid-1950s, when he briefly worked at extracting some rich copper-silver ore from the upper part of the complex. Then in the 1970s, the value of precious metals soared, and people from town again began spending their weekends puttering around old claims up in the hills. Sam had been holding on to the Eagle property and making plans for reworking the old tunnel systems. He had also made contact with a broker in Spokane, and before long he had a stock offering and enough capital to reopen Eagle Mine. He pulled out a brochure printed up by his promoters, which included two pages of salient information plus a photograph of a cart full of ore.

"Pretty spiffy, huh?" he remarked, tossing the brochure and map back into his steel box and pulling out a World War I doughboy helmet.

"By God," he said, "put this thing on and I'll take you down inside the mountain and show you what goes on in the real world." The protective gear sank down over my head like a soup bowl and lacked the small lamp attached to his own.

"No light," he growled into my ear. "You'll have to follow close."

The next instant he disappeared into the tunnel, and I had to skip along to follow the quavering light of his headlamp. The terrible noise of the compressor faded away, and we shuffled along in a black silence. The narrowness of the passageway forced us to walk single file, and up ahead the beam from Sam's headlamp was fading.

"Damn batteries," he complained, slapping his hard hat to bring the light back to life. "I've got a dozen good carbide lamps somewhere, but do you think I can find them?"

The temperature warmed a bit as we walked along the track, then leveled off to a clammy chill. Sam's wide body blocked the weak shine of his light, and I had to concentrate entirely on each step. Then a new stimulus entered my consciousness: water. At first we hit only puddles; since I had my boots on, I could blindly splash through the dips. But two hundred yards into the hill, the water collected into an ankle-deep stream of heartless cold, and I could feel liquid trickling down my boot tops.

"He'd better get that pump fixed, or we'll be flooded right out of here," Sam said. "How is it a grown man can't fix a simple pump?"

We trudged on slowly, heading further into the darkness, until I felt the floor and walls of the cave shudder around us.

"Step over to the side here," Sam directed, swinging his lamp beam to indicate a slight indentation in the sloping wall. The shudder increased, a light appeared, and around a sweeping corner crept the silhouette of a tiny air-powered railway car. A shadowy figure stood on the rear running board, maneuvering the contraption with twin control sticks.

The loud hiss of compressed air returned as Sam yelled questions at the driver about conditions farther up the tunnel.

"Hang it all!" he hollered. "It's just some dirt in the impeller. You two cowboys fix that pump and bring it back down here pronto. That means *now*."

The unearthly car slowly whistled off through the water. The rivulets that sparkled in its wake splashed like golden honey against the dark stone walls of the shaft. Sam forged ahead, and soon we came to an intersecting tunnel.

"All right," he said. "Here's where we leave the crosscut and head down the drift." He pointed into the passageway branching off to our left, explaining that it took its name from the way it drifted along a vein of ore rather than cutting straight through the mountain. He moved into the new tunnel, which was narrower than the one we had left, and disappeared around a turn. Hustling to catch up to the assurance of light, I suddenly bumped into his back.

"Watch yourself here," he warned. "This is the old Amazon shaft."

He tilted his head down. Just beyond the tips of our toes, the beam from his helmet disappeared into a bottomless black hole. I moved back very carefully.

"Don't worry," he said. "It's only two hundred feet deep. And only the first fifty are straight down—after that you'd just be sliding around and bumping off the walls." He chuckled at the thought. "A few weeks ago you could have had a nice swim down there, but we've got it all pumped out now." He lifted his head to point his headlamp in my direction. "O.K., step easy, this drift is taking a turn to the north."

We curled past the danger and walked ahead for another ten minutes, when suddenly the tunnel opened into a cathedral chamber thirty feet wide and almost as high. Tiny lights had been strung up for illumination, and square fir supports, still dripping with sap, arched beneath the vaulted rock. Across the huge room, four men worked together, excavating a new shaft. Sam pointed out that this particular shaft was being dug on an incline, rather than straight down. "That's called a winze," he instructed, "and it's headed for an ore zone about fifty feet in."

As we stood in the underground room, one of the workers came running over with a softball-sized rock, which he presented to the boss. "Hey Sam," he shouted. "Look at this!"

For less than ten seconds Sam studied the conglomerate glitter and sheen of the sample, then tossed it aside.

"Damn. We've got to teach you jokers some geology. But first maybe you should learn to put up a bent." He pointed to an unfinished post-and-beam support at the beginning of the new digs.

Three of the crewmen automatically poured out their intentions to complete the bent immediately. The fourth ended the discussion by returning to work with a resounding air hammer. Sam wandered over to the edge of the new shaft to observe the progress, and amid the confusion of bodies and noise his face was crossed with a look of pure enjoyment.

Behind him, two of the crewmen propped a painter's ladder against the incomplete bent. One of the men climbed to the top step and began whacking at a post with a two-pound maul, swinging it full overhead to drive the upright post level. His ladder came up just a little bit short. Its legs vibrated with each blow as his partner on the ground strained to hold it firmly in place.

Sam leaned so close to my ear that his hard hat glanced off mine. "Ladder stock," he said. "We need that ladder stock."

He turned and started back along the rails, casting a bear-like shadow against the stark walls of the underground room.

RAVEN TALK

*T*HEY CLOSED THE DUMP LAST WEEK. The *Chewelah Independent* carried a notice that the new sanitary landfill up on the Columbia River was ready to receive trash, which meant that the Chewelah town dump was officially closing.

"Huh," Lynn Walker exclaimed when he heard the news. "That's going to take some getting used to."

It was ugly, and its fires were illegal and dangerous, but the old dump was such an integral part of the local scene that it's hard to imagine the place without it. No burning regulations or toll-collecting booth marred the rummage-sale spirit of the Chewelah dump; it was open for business every day of the year, to any living organism hardy enough to find a place among the scavenging crowd. Located on a piney hillside that commanded a view of the town and surrounding farms, the dump's accumulated refuse had projected a broad, circular

tableland off the natural slope of the hill—an area that
expanded week by week as people backed up to its edge and
let fly with their rubble. Any trip to the mesa offered the twin
possibilities of pleasant conversation with seldom-seen
acquaintances and the discovery of secret valuables among
the scattered piles.

Two or three local families lived off remnants plucked
from other people's castoffs, and when a vehicle lumbered
backward into dumping position there was usually someone
around to assess the contents. Family groups came armed
with special rakes for sifting through the piles. Women and
children sorted out aluminum, while the men tackled cum-
bersome refrigerators and discarded sofas. Other people
weren't so picky; their rigs left in the evening full of rotten
barn lumber and twisted fencing. Many proper patrons lingered while unloading their trash, and seldom departed
completely empty-handed. One shaky stepladder in my own
yard has been back and forth to the mesa three times.

Living things thrived on the dump's myriad sources of
nourishment. Wildflowers of all kinds sprouted among the
refuse, and after a hard winter the first yellow buttercups and
pink phlox formed a welcome border around its edges.
Eurasian weeds seemed especially successful, and as spring
waned, those first delicate blooms gave way to pricklier plants
like knapweed, toadflax, woolly mullein, and bull thistle. But
even those tough soldiers did not stand alone: with summer's
heat a periphery of volunteer squash, tomatoes, and potatoes
shot up from the gravel to add more organic fuel to the mix.
The smell of hawthorn and mock orange combined with pine
pitch and assorted garbage odors to produce a heavy, intoxi-
cating air around the place. There always seemed to be a
hatch of bottle flies buzzing from a box of discarded canned
goods, or ground beetles marching away with last week's slimy
vegetables. Deer mice and wood rats skittered among the

cans, controlled by the horde of unwanted cats tossed out with people's trash. Distemper, target-practicing kids, and great horned owls in turn worked on the cat population.

Larger animals visited at night, drawn by the collection of bulky leftovers. On late trips home from town, I often caught a skunk in my headlights halfway up the hill and had to gear down to match its waddling pace until it veered into the woods. If I turned into the dump, there was much scrambling about, followed by the glow of eyeshines from protected vantages. By late summer there was always a juvenile bear that had grown accustomed to cruising the dump by night, inspiring neighbors to ride down and show off the bruin to friends. People naturally used such opportunities to kick up the day's glowing embers into sociable fires.

These fires caused the main complaints against the dump. Several days a month you could stand downtown at the stoplight and watch an ugly black swirl from burning tires course above the hillside. Local pyromaniacs made their whole year by lighting off tightly packed piles of garbage during the driest days of August, sending landowners into a panic and the volunteer fire department scurrying up the hill from town.

Since I had to drive past the dump every time I went to town, I developed a personal interest in the place. When quitting time rolled around on the day of closure, I made my way to an overlook above the mesa. Bulldozers had already raked the messy plateau clean of trash, then slathered the smoldering remains with load after load of fresh gravel. I watched a county crew string a heavy cable across the entrance, one that would not be easy to tear down. They rolled their bulldozer and front-end loader onto trailers and drove away into the afternoon haze.

With all finally quiet, I skidded down the slope and stepped cautiously onto the unfamiliar surface. Isolated plumes of smoke curled up from the bowels of the dump, hinting at the morass that lay beneath the gravel, but only the edges of the plain retained their black color and irregular shape. The tattered yellow hulk of a school bus hung on the rough slope. Beside it lay an ancient boiler tank, riddled with bullet holes and stuffed with the straw of a pack rat's nest. Hopping over the boiler, I picked my way along the lower level of the crescent where the slope ended below the county road. Tractor tires, car bodies, and half-buried plants spread into the woods. The bulldozer hadn't been able to fill in this last triangle where the steep slope met the road bank, and a dead calf lay stiff on the old ashes. I spent a few minutes staring at the contorted animal and all the rough debris that had tumbled down the incline during the big push, then sat down on a stump to enjoy the late afternoon.

One by one, the ravens began to appear, silent at first except for their squeaky wingbeats. They were returning to the dump to begin their regular dusk search through the trash; after feeding, they would roost in the yellow pines nearby. For as long as I had watched the dump, about forty of the scavengers had followed the same routine, gathering there each evening all through the winter and into their nesting season. As summer came on, many found other sources of food, and only extra-good pickings—an entire dead cow, or a root cellar's worth of ruined potatoes—could attract a big crowd of them back to the mesa.

The first birds circled, dipped down close, and lit on the coarse, even sand. More ravens flapped in from the rocky cliffs of Purple Flat Top, squawking down at their cohorts. Within half an hour three dozen birds were performing stunts over the tableland. Those that did land walked back and forth with cautious steps; there was none of the fierce posturing that usually accompanied their daily battles over food.

Finally a single white raven circled in. I jumped up without thinking; no matter how many times I saw this strange bird, I always wanted a better look. At my sudden movement, a black sentinel took off from one of the charred pines with a barrage of kworking screams. The white raven wheeled away and sailed over a green stand of new oats, disappearing into a dense fir grove on the far side of the field.

The white one had first appeared two summers before as a runt fledgling, and it took a while for me to believe my eyes. The bird showed itself only occasionally and was always the first to leave at any sign of human intrusion. At first I suspected that a regular raven had gotten mixed up with some lime or flour in the trash, but the dusting was awfully uniform and didn't wash off over time.

Curious for more glimpses of the apparition, I developed a habit of walking down to the dump each morning at dawn. I found that as the weather turned cold, the white raven's irregular visits grew more frequent and bold. Tom saw the bird on an early morning trip to town, then again in the middle of the day. Another neighbor sought me out to ask if she could have seen a seagull at the dump. From my own sightings, I was able to piece together a picture of the bird's peculiar coloring: black bill, black eyes, black feet, but feathers of a strong, clean white. This was no sickly albino any more than it was a common raven: the bird looked like some myth come alive.

Just before Christmas, a storm of fine, dry snow moved in from the north. Four inches of new powder muted the dump's smell of carnage and waste, transforming the junkyard into a serene plain. Magpies sat quietly in the alder sprouts along the west side of the flat. A few starlings whistled softly, bobbing through the snow without trying to feed, while the ravens muttered in low tones from roosting trees below the plateau. A cat tiptoed away from the hulk of an abandoned stove. Even though there was no food available, the ravens gradually descended from their pine trees to loiter on the clearing.

Above the flock a thin shadow moved within the light swirl of snowflakes. It was the white one, wheeling majestic and invisible against the pure white morning. As forest, sky, and raven mingled with the falling snow, the bird was revealed only by the jet black of its bill and feet. The ghost raven sailed a tight turn over the hollow, glided the length of the flat, then lit unnoticed on the ground. The black ravens stood silent in the middle of the parking area, motionless in the frozen desert. The white one began tugging at a flap of plastic that stuck up through the snow; suddenly an entire bag of bread jerked free. That small action broke the standing calm. Flapping loosely, the other birds ascended into the air, then joined into a unified boisterous flock that swept down and surrounded the bread bag. The white raven lifted into the air without a sound and disappeared beyond the cliffs, two magpies squawking at its tail.

I didn't see how such a harassed bird could possibly survive the winter and thought my doubts confirmed when no one saw it during March and April. But after the snow began to clear from the high country, a game warden swore that he had seen a white raven up in the national forest. I resumed my daily surveillance of the dump, and later in the month saw the bird twice. It seemed heavier, less skittish, and it stood among the group of black ravens instead of off to one side.

North of the dump, straight above my house, the crumbling arc of Purple Flat Top rose above the gravel outpourings left behind by the last glaciers. On hot summer afternoons, groups of ravens often wheeled in the thermals that steamed off its craggy brow: adults putting on their moves, youngsters imitating tight turns that would develop into the unlimited winged repertoire of their kind. The ravens screamed at every new trick or aggressive tail nip, honking off the brow of the cliffs as they mimicked sounds that drifted up from the barnyards below. The most dexterous birds skimmed the face of the quartzite, adjusting for the smallest indentations of arch and overhang as if tracing some ageless seam between feather and stone.

That summer the ghost raven joined its peers around Purple Flat Top, glistening white in the sun as the others glistened black. While I watched from my front yard, the white one ran the pinnacle course with a flurry of swirling turns and boinky sounds, executing a full barrel roll before it disappeared behind a column of stone. Other birds followed as the show stretched on through long summer evenings. When darkness settled, the flock sifted down into a clump of ragged lodgepoles at the base of the cliff, shaking flimsy trees with their crash landings. They ruffled, preened, then quickly dropped off to an evening's slumber.

Ravens talk in their sleep. With the entire flock roosted and sentries posted, odd noises began to burble out of the treetops. There were ducky quacks that recalled a cattail marsh, and mechanical sproings that could have come from the John Deere shop. Their mutterings coalesced into a pleasant low drone, drawing me toward the pines for companionship.

The ravens roosted along my driveway for more than a week, and if I stepped quietly and didn't get too close, they stayed put. But one evening I stumbled into the center of the group by mistake. A sentry bird straightened up with a croak, stirring the rest of the flock to life. Ravens crashed away from their crowns, brushing branches and veering wildly between the trees. The black force flapped through the forest, silent now except for the graceless crank of their heavy wings. Even in the poor light one of the escapees glowed white.

A few weeks after disturbing the ravens' night roost, I was at the grange filling my pickup with gas when a black Chevy

Nova backed toward me, offering a clear view of its reversed rear springs and fat tires. One of Lynn Walker's boys, almost hidden beneath an oversized cowboy hat, leaned out the driver's window.

"Hiya, Buzzy," I said. "How you been?"

"Not so bad. Hey, you know that white crow you see at the dump all the time?"

"Yeah," I answered slowly. "What about it?"

"You ever worry that somebody might shoot it or something?"

"I've thought about it, yeah."

"Well, you don't have to worry anymore. I think that bird's lying in the ditch up by our place. Somebody must've plugged it."

I made Buzzy pinpoint the location on the stretch of county road near Lynn's farm. I stopped pumping with the tank half full, paid inside, and zoomed back up the hill.

My pickup chugged around the S-turn past the dump, which was hidden in a pall of smoke and morning fog. I kept turning my head left and right, searching for whiteness. Beyond our driveway I slowed to a crawl. When a sparrow jumped out of a bare rosebush, I almost put the truck in the ditch.

There was no sign of a carcass along Lynn's cut field of barley, but on the next wide turn I caught a flash of white below a big pine. I skidded to a halt and leaped clear of the cab, then slowly approached the tree. It was a bird for certain, but the feathers didn't look quite right. They were short and ragged, not made for flying. With one touch, the identity of the corpse became clear: a decapitated white chicken had bounced out of someone's truck on the way to the dump.

After the chicken incident I began to wonder if the white raven might be getting a little too well known around town, but the bird remained a part of the regular raven flock right through the cold months. Whoever was first down the road in the morning usually got to watch it fly away from the trash, and with the coming of spring I began to wonder where the bird might breed and what its young would look like. Had it already happened without my knowing it, a nest full of naked piebald offspring stuffed into some hidden pocket of the quartzite cliffs? In any case, the dump's closure would put the white one on its summer schedule in a hurry. Once that last dead calf below the road bank was consumed, the tenants would begin to take their leave.

When the raven flock returns next fall, they'll find knap-weed and sweet yellow clover, and new cottonwood sprouts where the gravel coating is thin. I can imagine there will be a few messy piles of illegal trash, but they won't add up to enough sustenance for scavenger birds to winter here, and my habit of sneaking around at dawn to watch their movements must end. The valley below still looks the same, but no matter how hard I stare into that dark green grove of Douglas firs beyond the oat field, there's no trace of white among the crowns.

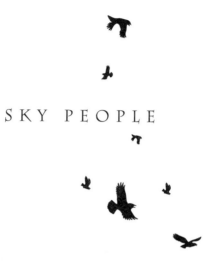

SKY PEOPLE

I WAS A LITTLE LATE FOR OUR RENDEZVOUS downtown and met Pauline Pascal Flett as she emerged from the restaurant carrying four cups of coffee and a large white sack. Pauline's mother, Selena, followed close behind—small, almost shrunken, but quite beautiful in a clean shift. Selena's long hair hung straight down her back, shining with tones of silver and gray, and her skin glowed around deep wrinkles of age. When Pauline introduced us, Selena answered with a barely audible "hello" and slipped into the passenger seat of Pauline's Buick.

Pauline was a Spokane Indian woman with a full, expressive face and a determined mind. As head of the Spokane Language Center she had immersed herself in researching and compiling the linguistic culture of her people. Fewer than a hundred tribal members still spoke fluent Spokane, so Pauline's project had a certain urgency.

Today we were going to visit an eighty-two-year-old woman named Alice Abrahamson who had grown up in the Colville Valley and never moved to a reservation.

After a short jaunt down a dirt road, we pulled into the driveway of a small brick house with new porches front and rear and half of a pumpkin-orange paint job. Pauline crossed the wooden porch, rapped on the screen door, and walked in. Selena and I followed her into an atmosphere of cool, dark security.

"Aunt Alice?" Pauline called, raising her voice over the television in the living room.

A stocky woman in a dark blue print dress moved slowly over to greet us. Alice had a round face and owlish features; her steel gray hair was tightly wound and pinned close to her head. She used a cane for support, and the stretched skin on the back of her gripping right hand rippled with an intricate map of color and texture.

"I'm watching my show," she said. "Come in the sitting room, here."

Her show was *The Price is Right.* She turned down the sound a bit and descended into a big overstuffed easy chair, facing the screen, while Pauline passed around the coffee and maple bars from the sack. Selena sank into another soft chair in a dark corner, leaving me a rocker in the middle of the floor. Windows opened out of the north and west walls of Alice's living room, but heavy curtains remained drawn over them. An insistent summer sun behind these curtains and the gray glow of the TV screen provided the room's only light. A few small family photos, a portrait of Jesus, and a horse painted on velvet decorated the walls.

After we were all settled, Pauline outlined the general information she wanted—names, dates, and places that Alice might remember from her childhood—and mentioned that I would like to hear any bird or animal legends that she and

Selena might recall. Later on I was going to try to help Pauline connect modern English names with the creatures and plants of the tales, so that she could use them in teaching the Spokane language to reservation schoolchildren. Pauline fished a recorder out of her purse and punched in a cassette, and the three women slowly began to talk.

Alice grew up on a farm near Chewelah shortly after the turn of the century. In those days the Colville Valley was a wet place, covered by seasonal bogs and lakes; small boats were a standard form of transportation. The valley was populated by a wide variety of native bands: Chewelahs, Kalispels, Spokanes, and Flatheads, all of whom spoke variations of the Interior Salish language. There were French-Canadians from the fur trade era, who taught her people French words for new animals they had brought with them, like roosters and pigs. And there were many recent immigrants, mostly Germans and Swedes. The river ran clear, and crayfish were a favorite treat. Alice's grandfather trapped muskrat around the lakes and ermine and marten in the surrounding hills. A key change to the look and feel of the valley took place around 1910 with the dredging of the Colville River. This channelization controlled spring flooding and opened up large areas of the valley for farming, but altered the distribution of native plants and animals forever. I asked Alice if there had been elk in the valley before the dredging project. Had she heard wolves at night? She shrugged and returned to her discussion of names and dates.

Alice did mention one root plant, called wild carrot, that had been a favorite with the local people. She said that the plant had gradually disappeared after the dredging. Pauline and I tried to work a description out of her, so that we could determine the exact species. As we talked, Selena suddenly perked up. She knew a story, and it involved both wolves and the wild carrot.

There were four wolf brothers who had a particular fond-
ness for this wild carrot. When its season came around, they
handed their sister a good dogwood digging stick and told her
to go and gather its roots. Little Sister went out the first day
but came back with only a few small, misshapen roots. The
wolf brothers didn't like that. They sent her out again, but on
the second day she didn't do any better.

Then on the third day, Little Sister came home with a
whole sackful of the wild carrots, and when the brothers
asked her what had happened, she just smiled and said that
she had finally found a good spot. On the fourth and fifth
days Little Sister again came home with sackfuls of roots, and
the brothers decided that something strange was going on.
They studied the roots that their sister had brought home,
and . . .

"What was it?" Selena stopped her narrative, stuck on the
botanical detail—there was something about those roots. She
and Alice pondered together for a few moments, then Alice
asked if wild carrots weren't the ones with the stringy core.

"Ah, yes," nodded Selena, the memory flooding back. "I
know now."

The four wolf brothers studied the roots that their sister
was bringing home; each root had a long silver hair right
down its middle. This set the wolves to thinking, and the
next day one of the brothers followed Little Sister out into
the forest when she left to look for wild carrots.

Little Sister walked straight down a long trail and
bumped into Grizzly Bear. To Brother Wolf's surprise, the two
acted as if they had met before. Together they began to search
for carrots, and in no time Grizzly Bear had scraped up a
whole sackful of them to present to Little Sister. Whenever
she wasn't looking, he would pluck one of the silver hairs
from his body and hide it in the root he had just dug up.
Grizzly Bear had a plan: he figured the wolf brothers would

find the long hairs stuck in the roots and suspect that Little Sister must be gathering her daily food in some very strange manner. They would follow her out to the woods, discover that she was meeting secretly with Grizzly Bear, and make her marry him, which is what old Grizzly Bear wanted. And that is exactly what happened.

Alice nodded in enjoyment at Selena's version of the story, and they described again the long silver hairs, like single strings, at the core of each wild carrot.

"They don't grow around here anymore," mused Alice, "but we all used to eat them when we were children."

Pauline mentioned a couple of locations where she knew that the wild carrots could still be found, and we decided that when they bloomed next month we would go out and try to identify them.

Selena and Alice haggled about details of the short legend, sometimes speaking a few phrases of Spokane to each other. The sounds of the native language were soft and musical. The bewildering glottal stops and accents I had seen on paper in Pauline's office were transformed into a burbling stream of conversation.

Pauline steered them toward the subject of Spil ya, the coyote of Spokane legend. She was interested in a story that concerned Spil ya and a special drying rack. Selena had been trying to sort out the details of the story by sleeping with a tape recorder beside her bed, but so far she had remembered only the bare outline. After listening to Selena, Alice closed her eyes for a few moments, then presented her own rendition.

Spil ya was watching a huge bull elk walk along a ridge one afternoon. He had not eaten for many days, and he really wanted a taste of that good elk meat. Spil ya approached the elk and yelled:

"Watch out, Brother Elk! You're about to step on a sharp thorn! Don't take that step!"

Brother Elk looked down and saw a little green cricket—
the kind that has a long spine growing out of its tail. Startled,
Elk tripped and stumbled right off the rocky ridge and rolled
down the slope. He landed upside down, stuck on the wide
spread of his own antlers.

Spil ya followed poor Elk down the slope and quickly finished him off. He and Cricket agreed to divide the meat,
since Cricket had helped in the hunt. Cricket could not possibly eat all that meat at once, so Spil ya built a rack out of
tree limbs, sliced up the elk, and placed all the meat on the
rack to dry. Then he fell asleep.

While he was napping, all the different birds and animals
that lived around there came up and started to devour the
fresh elk meat . . . .

"Wait a minute," broke in Selena. "I remember one way
it goes now, but he wasn't sleeping." And Selena took over
the telling.

Spil ya was sitting down to guard his meat, and all the
birds and animals of the forest arrived to start eating. Spil ya
tried to jump up and chase them away, but he was stuck in
his seat.

Selena looked inquisitively at Alice, who by now was on
the edge of her big soft chair. But Alice shook her head; she
wasn't exactly sure what caused Spil ya's immobility.

In any case, Spil ya had to sit and watch while the creatures of the forest consumed every bit of his elk meat. After
feasting, they were so stuffed that they all instantly fell asleep.
And suddenly Spil ya found that he could move again.

Alice drew a quick breath, seeming to remember the
moment when the tables turned. She chuckled as Selena
continued her narrative.

That's when Spil ya really got into some mischief. He
walked over to the drying rack, where nothing was left but
the grease from the elk meat. He dipped his paws in that

grease, and when he touched the animals with his greasy paws, bizarre things happened. Spil ya twisted the bill of one of the birds, and the beak remained twisted up and down. He dipped his paws full of grease and rubbed them all over Crow and Magpie, leaving them black and shiny. Spil ya drew circles, he made stripes, he decorated many familiar animals with the elk fat. But . . .

Selena looked at Alice again. What was the next animal that Spil ya marked with his wonderful grease? Badger maybe? Or Skunk?

"Well, shoot," I broke in. "The bird with the twisted bill has to be a crossbill."

All three women looked at me as if they had forgotten I was in the room and then burst out laughing. The mention of birds led Alice and Selena into a discussion of the bright goldfinches that had been going after the thistles in the fields below Alice's house.

"Do those crossbills chatter like the little goldfinches?" Selena wanted to know.

"Not like that," I said. "It's more steely, like 'Kip kip . . . Kip kip . . . Kip'."

Tittering with amusement, Selena and Alice fell into the quick rhythms of a Spokane exchange, and I heard the unmistakable song of a meadowlark flutter up from their words. I named the bird immediately; Pauline spelled it out for me on a piece of paper: *wawickwle*. Pauline, Alice, and Selena all encouraged me to say it. Each lady's repeated pronunciation sounded off subtle variations of a meadowlark song.

"Wawickwle is going to tell you some news," said Alice. "Each morning, spring and summer, we step outside and Meadowlark tells us what's going on."

"Yes, yes," said Selena. "Just the other day I was standing at my back door and Meadowlark piped up: 'That's sure an ugly old sweater you're wearing today!'"

The meadowlark's name, so closely mimicking its intricate call, caught my interest, and I asked Pauline if she knew of any other names like it.

"Well, there's *hmis hmis*," she said, pronouncing the double syllable with a low coo that sounded just like the call of a mourning dove. "You know *hmis hmis* don't you?"

Selena's smile faded, and she related a tale of the day a certain tribe broke for their winter camp. The chief had made up his mind very suddenly, and the people had to gather up their possessions and move right away. One widow's son was off in the woods hunting rabbits, and when he returned to camp, there was no one around. The boy became frightened and began to cry forlornly, "Hmis . . . hmis hmis," which is Spokane for "Momma."

Spil ya happened to be passing nearby in the woods when he heard the pitiful cries of the boy. For some reason the sobs angered Spil ya, and he approached the lonely child.

"So!" declared Spil ya. "You want to cry for your mother? I'll help you do it."

With a wave of Spil ya's paw, the boy was transformed into a mourning dove. He flew off the ground and perched on the branch of a tree, where he continued his sad cadence.

"Hmis hmis . . . hmis hmis hmis."

Her story finished, Selena went on to tell us that a few days earlier she had awakened and heard a mourning dove outside her window—she imitated the call "hmis hmis." On that morning she just had to cry because the dove sounded so pitiful.

Alice stood up and served coffee all around. Sneaking a glance at Pauline's watch, I realized that the morning was almost gone. Through second cups of coffee, the three women spoke of goings-on around the tribal headquarters at Wellpinit. Then they delved into the problems of a mutual friend who lived over on the Columbia River, an older woman who seemed to be losing her humor and her memory at the same time. The thought of her disintegration circled the conversation back to tribal lore. As Pauline popped a third cassette into her tape recorder, Alice lamented that much of what she had been told as a child was forgotten after the strict, narrow focus of education at the reservation school. Pauline said that when she was little, everyone around her spoke Spokane, and Selena had taught her the location and preparation of many medicinal plants. Yet by the time she graduated from high school, she had forgotten every leaf and only recently had begun to relearn the intricate natural history of the area.

Selena agreed that the school had pushed a lot from her mind also, but as a child she was lucky enough to live with two aunts who loved to tell stories. During the short days of winter, these ladies would sit the children down and dip into a store of legends covering every conceivable subject. The aunts created a world that still existed outside, around the cabin on dark winter nights. But as time passed, Selena had trouble remembering the sequence and details of the different stories. Her mind was like a salmon floating in its spawning stream: weary and cautious, yet still capable of quick, graceful flashes of movement.

We sat quietly for several minutes while Selena contemplated those nights with her aunts. When I noticed Pauline shuffling things in her purse as if making ready to leave, I realized that I was not ready to go yet, not at all. Groping for an excuse to keep the women talking, I asked them about an early diary I had read that described Kalispel Indians living in the Colville Valley. Yet the Kalispel Reservation was located in the Pend Oreille Valley, across the mountains east from Chewelah. Before white people arrived, was this valley Kalispel or Spokane territory?

"Oh sure, Kalispels were over here," answered Alice. "I'm half Kalispel myself. This one branch of the people went back and forth over the trail by Chewelah Peak all the time, like they couldn't decide where they wanted to live. You know that story about Frog? With his eyes growing way up on top of his head?"

Frog doesn't know where he's going half the time. He hops up the Flowery Trail till he gets to the pass at Chewelah Peak and looks down, but his high eyes are looking right back where he came from. "Say!" he says. "That's a fine-looking valley. I'm going to hop down there and live." But when he gets down, he's either in the wrong valley or right back where he started.

"Which is it?" asked Alice. "Anyway, he keeps going back and forth, always seeing behind himself."

"I remember now," said Selena. "Not which way Frog went—I never did understand what he was seeing. I remember something about Coyote and that trouble he was in over the drying rack."

When Spil ya ran his claws down little Chipmunk's back, the magic grease from the drying rack caused those long stripes to remain forever. And Coon's dark eye mask, weren't the circles drawn with that same grease? And wasn't there something about Sucker?

"Oh, no, Mom, not Sucker," Pauline broke in. "Aren't you thinking about the time Sucker fell from the sky? About the war with the Sky People?"

Although Selena and Alice immediately recalled the story Pauline referred to, neither could come up with a satisfactory explanation for the origin of the Sky People. According to Selena, they were simply up there; it was back in the time before people, when animals lived together as equals. Of course, Spil ya was around; in fact, he had only recently brought fire into the world. Then the Sky People came down and stole the fire, and the creatures on earth once again huddled in cold and darkness. They had to get their fire back in order to live right, so they found a champion . . .

"I'm not so sure," interrupted Alice. "Maybe they found Spil ya."

"No, no," Selena said. "I don't think it was Spil ya."

Whoever the champion was, he drew back his bow and shot an arrow high, high into the air, and that arrow went up and stuck right in the bottom of the clouds. The marksman drew back his bow again and fired another arrow. Up it flew, high in the air, until it struck the feathered end of the first arrow and hung down from it. Over and over the archer shot his arrows, and each tip lodged in the previous feathered end, until there was a chain of arrows stretching from the clouds to the earth.

Then all the earth dwellers went aloft to get back their precious fire from the Sky People. Everyone was eager to go; they all scrambled up the chain of arrows. Grizzly Bear wanted to join them but was afraid there might not be anything for him to eat up in the land of the Sky People, so he packed several baskets of food and picked a big basket of hawthorn berries before starting the journey.

He started to climb, hand over hand, one arrow after the other, heading for the deck of clouds. But Grizzly Bear was so big, and his baskets so heavy, that just as he reached the clouds, the arrow he was holding snapped loose from the others. Grizzly Bear tried to grab another arrow for a new hold, but it also broke away, and he fell. He clutched at more and more arrows as he went down, but each one came away in his paws. Before long, Grizzly Bear was sitting back on earth, and the chain of arrows was demolished.

Now all the other creatures were trapped in the clouds with no way to get down. And Selena's memory left most of them up there, because she couldn't recall how each one escaped. She knew that many creatures gained their forms as we know them from that trip to the sky, just as Spil ya completed the appearance of many animals at the drying rack. But which ones?

Pauline remembered. Sucker was one of the animals stranded in the land of the Sky People. He couldn't find any way down, so finally he leaped into space. After a long fall he landed hard on a bed of sharp pine needles. The needles were driven in all over Sucker's body, and that's why he has so many bones to pick out when you try to eat him.

Sucker's story jarred Selena just enough; she was smiling even before he hit his bed of pine needles. "One more," she said, "and then we should go home."

Little Bat was high in the clouds, but he was more like a mouse than the bat we know today. He had no wings, just four short legs, and he was carrying a small blanket. Bat scurried around and gathered some broken arrow pieces left from Grizzly Bear's plunge. He poked them into his blanket as struts, then held the blanket over his shoulders and leaped out of the clouds. For a long time Bat floated gently underneath the blanket parachute on his way back to earth. And when he drifted close to the ground, there was Spil ya watching him descend.

"That's very good, Brother Bat," Spil ya said with admiration. "From now on your blanket with the broken arrow struts will be a part of you, and you will fly anywhere you want. You will still look like a mouse, but now you'll be a bird as well."

As she finished her story, Selena seemed to shrink deep into her cushion. Moving her hands slowly, she lifted a black, loose-knit afghan that hung behind her on the easy chair. For a moment she held it over her head, her small arms crooked like newfound wings. Alice leaned forward and patted the television to show her approval.

"All right, Mom," said Pauline, smiling. "Let's head back to the river."

She led us slowly from Alice's dark living room, outside into the blinding sunlight of the hot afternoon.

FOSSIL BOWL

A SHORT NOTICE HIDDEN ON THE regional page of the Spokane newspaper caught my eye: botanical fossils from the Clarkia area collected by Professor Charles J. Smiley would be on display in the University of Idaho Library for the next ten days. The specimens included exotic Asian conifers as well as a large selection of familiar hardwoods native to eastern North America. I read the notice three times over, trying to grasp the idea of oaks and beeches flourishing in the dry mountain habitats of the Inland Northwest, then phoned the university's geology department. It took a while, but a determined secretary finally located Professor Smiley. He sounded cheerful, even enthusiastic, and suggested that I drop by his laboratory after lunch the next day.

I arrived in Moscow just after noon and found Smiley's secretary, who directed me toward a long basement connected to the main building's steam plant. I ducked down a half-flight of steps and entered a cavernous expanse of shelves and desks. Inside the room flat hunks of mudstone littered every available surface, creating an atmosphere thick with the smell of dried mud and rotting vegetable matter. Embossed on many of the hard clay samples were the imprints of leaves and ferns, their delicate patterns dancing in the poor light as I stepped cautiously between the tables.

Professor Smiley was working in the rear of the shed, wielding a large pair of bolt cutters. He wore brown corduroys, a checkered shirt topped with a string tie, and a black and white houndstooth jacket. His body was taut as he leaned into the effort of his work.

"Ahhhh!" he grunted, snapping his big nippers closed on a dinner-plate-sized sample of thick dried mud. The cut piece tumbled onto the floor. Smiley dove down and snatched it up, examining its edges closely.

"Here we are, right here." He shoved the sample into my hands. "Have a look at these."

A series of laminations cut across the end of the clay section, bedded much like fine slate in a quarry. I touched the seams with my fingers before introducing myself. Professor Smiley responded with a quick nod, and I asked what would happen if someone split the laminations.

"That's just it," he answered, banging the piece down among thousands of others on a long table. He picked up a ball-peen hammer in one hand and a wide coal chisel in the other. One smart tap on the central seam of the clay fragment produced a resonant ring; with a second peck the chunk opened like a book. Professor Smiley separated the two halves and turned over the first section with his quick fingers, revealing the clear impression of a maple leaf inscribed in the mud. Like an operator in a shell game, he rotated his palm to disclose the other half of the tablet.

Imbedded in the clay was an actual maple leaf, perfectly preserved down to the orange color of a New England fall. As we watched, a remarkable thing happened: fresh oxygen pouring in on the long-preserved cells of the leaf began to age it from the moment of its autumn drop several epochs ago. My mouth dropped open as the lively sunset hue faded to a muddy brown and finally died to a lifeless charcoal.

"The really perplexing thing," Smiley continued, as if working out a conversation we had started last week, "is not what we've gained by exposing this leaf, but what we've lost by choosing that particular lamination to put the chisel to. There might be something stuck between each of these other layers, but now they're too thin to pull off cleanly. I never know what I'm missing in this place."

Relaxing his intense concentration, the professor put the two pieces of split clay down on the table.

"Let's go back," he said, "so you can see how I got so wrapped up in all this."

Smiley had started his career as a plant paleontologist specializing in the Cretaceous period. To illustrate, he uncovered a black globule that he had hauled out of a gold mine in Ecuador. It was about the size of a bowling ball, shot through with fossilized ocean shells.

"That's where I started, right there," he said, fingering an ammonite in the dark globe. "About a hundred million years ago."

In the late 1960s, Smiley was sidetracked into a project that involved late Miocene flora—specimens only a quarter the age of his gold sample. One day in 1972 a man phoned him from Clarkia, on the St. Maries River. The caller said he had been bulldozing a motorcycle racetrack when funny things began spilling out of the bank on the third turn. The professor drove out for a look and immediately recognized the very Miocene communities he had been working on, represented to a far greater extent than he ever could have imagined.

This bonanza had once been a forest growing along the edge of a lake. Flora and fauna fell into the lake, sank into stagnant, oxygen-poor water at the bottom, and were gradually covered by layers of a peculiar local clay. Drainage outwash and occasional floods varied the thickness of the annual clay layers but did not harm the vestiges of forest sealed between them. The structural tissues of the maple leaf we had exposed remained unchanged from the fall day long ago when the leaf sailed down into the lake.

After a few hundred years, many feet of the humus-clay mixture had silted into the lake. Then a slight shift in the local climate closed the system down. Over the next twenty million years, nothing of significance disturbed the stacks of embedded vegetation. Once the ancient scene was exposed, all Professor Smiley had to do was back a dump truck up to the third turn, work a representative cut off the bank, and start chiseling.

Smiley could see I was hooked. He wandered through his tables, touching this piece, turning that one over, reworking the process by which he had identified all the different kinds of trees. At first they seemed to include the entire spectrum of southern hardwoods, from lowland cypress to mountain magnolias, but he discovered that his species didn't quite match up chemically with our modern forms. That made no difference to me.

The sight of that crumbling gray leaf sent me back to the forests where I had grown up, at the edge of the southern Appalachians. In the presence of the leaves, I was fourteen years old again, standing beside a stacked firewood pile, trying to figure out how our neighbor James Richard could read a clear message in every sawed stick in the cord. James pointed out details in the end grains—"See how punky this tulip tree grows? That's what makes it good to hold a rope on a snatch block." He ran his fingers along the different barks—"Only dogwood is so broken up, like a cob of corn after you've chewed the kernels off." He inhaled deeply of certain pieces through his broad nostrils—"Catch the bitter in this cherry. And mind that the smell gets stronger when you saw into it." James tried to make me understand that each piece, even stacked into a pile, retained the character of the living tree. When spring came and the leaves burst out in their unfathomable masses, I could remember all of James's names.

"And it's not just leaves that we're looking at," Professor Smiley said.

He picked up a clay tablet that bore the imprint of a fish slightly smaller than my hand. I reached for it, but he had already replaced the fish fossil on the bench and moved on, pointing this time to a small irregularity pressed into the mitten-shaped leaf of a sassafras tree. I had to look closely to recognize it as an insect. When I focused on the squeezed leaf, a voice from the cricket family rang in my head: "katy did," singing away on a summer's night in my childhood. Two of the crickets joined in a duet: "Ka Ka ty did ty did did," and I turned over in my sleep, flinging away damp sheets in the thick humidity of the night. More of their kind joined the chorus until the entire swamp behind our house roared with a crescendo—"KATYDIDKATYDIDKATYDIDKATY-DID"—and I sat straight up in bed, wondering what could possibly have awakened me, as the chorus died away to nothing and the stifling blackness was silent again.

Professor Smiley changed continents on me now, reaching into a battered cupboard and pulling out the imprint of a dawn redwood, the mythical *Metasequoia*.

"Lost to botanists for generations," he announced, "to reappear only in the depths of China. But it turns out that specimens have been buried on the third turn of our local racetrack the entire time."

He exchanged the redwood tablet for a small glass vial which contained another sort of conifer, a tiny fir seedling washed into the Miocene lake and flattened by the weight of drifting silt. Smiley had laid open one clay specimen and discovered the seedling intact, root system and all. He dropped the sprout into water and watched it puff back up to three dimensions, then sent it away for examination. A specialist identified the seedling as an Asian fir presently existing only in the Yellow River drainage of China.

"Do you get this?" Smiley asked me. "We are looking at a forest that contained species which today are found only in central China and the temperate zones of North America. Together. Right here."

During a relatively warm period of the earth's history, this pleasant community had been sustained by moisture that blew in unimpeded from the Pacific Ocean. Then the Cascade Range gradually rose up and captured the wet clouds. A global cooling cycle finished off the deciduous forest and gave rise to the dry, cold coniferous mix we know today.

At this point Smiley reached his unclassified table. One tablet contained a leaf that looked very much like it had fallen off a beech tree, but instead of the familiar nut produced by the present-day species, a conelike strobile protruded from below the leaf stem, plain as day. No one else had published records of a tree like this. Smiley said he wanted to name it *pseudofagus*—"looks like a beech." I laughed with delight at the simplicity of his approach, and the professor was right with me.

"Pretty good, huh? How do you name things that no one ever saw? Or how about this one?"

Smiley selected another sample from the mystery table. This, too, was obviously a leaf, but not one from any of the tree families that we had seen so far. It had lobes, and teeth, and murky indentations that didn't match anything James Richard had ever planted in my memory. "No record remotely like it, fossil or living," Smiley said. "So where do we go to find a place for it?"

The vagaries of his basement full of fossils seemed to excite rather than distress the professor. After struggling for five years to catalog that first dump-truck load from turn three at the racetrack, his job had evolved into that of a coordinator. Someone had to identify specimens and pass them safely along to scientists around the world who might tease more information from them. Someone had to perform the more difficult trick of bringing together people from specialties like dendrology and entomology, taxonomy and biochemistry. In the long run, Smiley knew, it would take a lot of cooperation to understand the workings of the whole system at Clarkia. Even now, there were lipid researchers in England doing fascinating things with fats extracted from the leaves. A genetic chemist had apparently just isolated viable DNA from fossilized cypress needles. The technology of dating techniques was changing so fast, it was hard to keep up. And if a single stray bird feather had floated down to be pressed into one of those millions of leaves . . .

"Dr. Smiley?"

The professor's secretary was calling from the basement door above us. "Dr. Smiley? You haven't forgotten your three o'clock meeting?"

Professor Smiley laid down his bolt cutters and rearranged his string tie.

"Course I haven't," he called up to the doorway. Turning to me, he said, "Have to run. You can stick around here for a while if you want. Be careful though, and don't touch anything that's already cracked open." He hustled up the stairs and disappeared.

Alone in the laboratory, I stopped beside a pile of unsplit chunks of mudstone and hefted one of them in my hands. I wet two fingers in my mouth and drew them down one edge to reveal the pattern of even layers. Resisting the temptation to take up hammer and chisel, I returned the sample to its spot on the crowded bench. Right beside it lay the little fish that Professor Smiley had not quite let me see. It was a sun-fish of some sort, like the first finned creature I ever tried to catch. I recalled the feeling as my Uncle John grabbed away my cane pole and flicked its end so that worm and bobber drifted lazily toward a sunken snag. The bobber stuttered, then dove. Uncle John jerked the pole back to set the hook, lifting it clear of the muddy water, and I was astonished to see that a glittering bream now writhed at the end of the line. The fish gasped as it landed on shore; it lay still for one second and then took off flopping.

"Get it, Uncle John!" I squealed.

"It's not mine to get," he said. "That's your fish."

I dove for it, hitting the slippery mud. The spiny fin along the bream's back speared my palm. I flinched away, and the fish kept flopping. I looked up at Uncle John, desperate now for help.

"Your fish."

The bream threw the hook and flopped down the slick bank back toward the pond. I took off after it, chased by Uncle John's chuckles.

The bream flicked its silver body twice, three times, flung itself clear of a tuft of slimy grass, and splashed back into the reddish brown liquor of the pond.

Outside the building, I found my truck in the student parking lot and caught the highway east toward Clarkia. The road wound up into the hills, skirting the boundary of the St. Joe National Forest through pockets of big western white pines. The best grew ramrod straight off the steep hillsides, their trunks without taper or branch for sixty feet. Powdery blue green needles made groves across the canyon stand out like sailing clouds. The good humus and clay left behind after the Miocene must now be nourishing these giants.

When I pulled over on a turnout to inspect some of the trees, I found myself at the entrance to an abandoned commercial clay pit. Its surface was carpeted by a pygmy forest of coniferous seedlings that had sprouted to life, then stopped growing abruptly when their roots couldn't break through the clay hardpan. Several trenches dug by potters were filled with water; I knelt down beside the closest one and plunged both hands into the slick goo, feeling the airless seal formed by a few inches of clay over a single leaf on the shore of an ancient lake.

Just beyond the clay pit, the highway crested a summit, then fell in beside the quiet beginnings of the St. Maries River. The town of Clarkia sat in the high valley there, among the green shades of a mountain July. Two miles south of town I came upon a large metal sign: FOSSIL BOWL RACE-TRACK. I peeked through a wooden fence at a rough snack shed and gnarled infield. A distinctive clay track wound through a series of bumps and turns, one of them carved around a low bank of exposed substrate. Even from a distance, I could make out row after row of bedded laminations along the face of the bank. And even without Professor Smiley nearby, I could hear the faint calls of living plants, resting for now between those tightly pressed seams. Behind a set of small wooden bleachers, the moveable plastic letters of another signboard announced:

MOTOCROSS/LAST WEEK IN JULY/DON'T MISS OUT!

SIGN

CROWELL RIDGE IS A ROUGH, EIGHT-mile crescent that connects two mountain peaks in northeastern Washington, very near the border with British Columbia. Because of its stark exposure and ancient geology, the ridge presents a variety of alpine delicacies. On an early fall day, Tom Burke and I scrambled up a trail along the rocky southern slope of the ridge, breaking out of a closed canopy of fir and hemlock into a haunting, open forest of fire-killed winter pines. Remnant snags stuck up like spears, seared in a fire almost half a century before but still standing. Beside the bare ghosts, clumps of living whitebarks gained in stature, draped with scaly bark and straggly, thick-needled branches right up to their crowns.

Within this forest, complete silence and a cool temperature suspended the September morning. I took five steps, turned in a circle around one gnarled snag, and touched its naked trunk. The aged surface of the dead pine's thick butt felt like polished ivory. Corkscrew lines running through the wood revealed a tortuous growth, and the stunted tree stretched only thirty feet into the sky. I circled it again and almost stumbled over my hiking companion, who was scrabbling through the rocks on his hands and knees.

"Watch your step," he said.

Producing a pair of long tweezers from his backpack, he pinched them dexterously around the shell of a dead land snail. He reached for a collecting bottle, unscrewed the lid, and dropped his catch into a solution of ethyl alcohol and glycerin.

Burke worked as a biologist for the Colville National Forest; over the past few seasons he had been gathering information on the gastropods of northeastern Washington. No one had ever studied snails in this area before, and it turned out there were lots of them. Several species lapped over from eastern and western ranges, and it was not always easy to recognize the different kinds. Burke sat down on the slope, holding his snail of the moment up to the autumn sunlight. The shell took the form of a swollen disk about the size of a nickel, bleached as white as the dead pines. Its spiral pattern wound to a distinct raised point, and an oval entrance opened off the left side. Beside my knee, nestled in the bunchgrass, lay another shell just like it. Within five minutes of concentrated searching—noses down and eyes focused— we had picked up three more.

"Sometimes a fire will do that," Burke said. "The heat drives all the snails to the surface and cooks them. You go out on some burns and see snails all over the place, but if the fire was too hot, the shells might be nothing but ash— one touch and they turn to dust. Then on another burn, like this one here, you have a census that is preserved almost forever. Unless, of course, one species cooks to ash before another."

We paced around beneath the whitebarks for a few minutes longer, until Burke was convinced that the snail remains around this particular site all belonged to the same species. Then we took off walking again, methodically scanning the opposite slopes. The day was fair, the wind light. The jumble of ridges that ran toward Canada and Idaho seemed ready to burst with color—the vine maples were already deep red, the willows light yellow. The scattered tamaracks, just beginning to turn, showed both gold and green. Squares of clear-cut forest broke up the solid canopy of trees, and we counted eight elk and five mule deer browsing in one big scar.

The elevation of the mountain peaks that were visible from the ridge ascended to six or seven thousand feet, and any one of them could be climbed in a day: these were mountains with people in them. The first European explorers found that the local Spokane and Kalispel tribes visited the highest meadows to gather medicinal plants, and scraped red and yellow ochres from time-worn deposits to use as paint. Since then even the most remote sections had been touched by prospectors' picks, logging machines, and the toughest of the homesteading lot. This morning in the high clear air we could occasionally hear the steady *ka-chunk ka-chunk ka-chunk* of the Metaline Falls cement plant far below us, crushing raw limestone into cement.

Our legs loosened up in the mild fall weather, and within an hour we broke past timberline onto the narrow, crumbling hogback of Crowell Ridge. We were almost halfway between Crowell Mountain and Gypsy Peak when the trail skirted the top of a glacial cirque. Tumbled boulders cascaded toward a small oval of wetland vegetation in the bottom of the bowl. Burke whipped out his binoculars to study the different shades of green.

"Whoa," he said. "Bet there're some good plants growing around that little pond. I wonder how long it would take us to climb down there and back out?"

A sharp whistle sounded from within the cirque. I immediately began to scan for a goshawk circling below us, but Burke was not so sure. He closed his eyes and tucked his chin down, as if he were trying to remember something. Another whistle sounded, high and shrill. I couldn't locate any bird swooping through the air.

"I think that's a marmot," said Burke. "A hoary marmot."

I had heard hoary marmots whistle from really grand places—Going to the Sun Highway in Glacier National Park, Kicking Horse Pass in Alberta, and Ross Pass through the North Cascades—but I had never associated the sleepy woodchuck with these smaller mountains close to home. And yet, on a map, Crowell Ridge sits in the middle of a triangle described by those three points.

"I think that's what it is," Burke nodded. "And I don't think there's any record of hoary marmots from this part of the Selkirks. The closest one I know of would be from the other side of Priest Lake. But there's no reason they couldn't be here. No reason at all. Let's go down and see if we can get a look at it."

It was a couple of hours before we made it back out of the cirque. We were bushed, battered, and had not seen any trace of a marmot. The only thing on either of our minds was lunch, so we sat down right on the trail to eat. A flock of chickadees, twittering with energy, gathered in the nearby lodgepoles, and I whistled to try and lure them closer. The whistle faded in my mouth as the air was filled with a deep, mournful howl—a single, loud, drawn-out sound, so close that it reverberated in the space around us.

Neither of us breathed for thirty seconds after the noise finally ceased. The howl had been distinct and quite beautiful, but I wasn't altogether certain I had heard it. Burke also had a confused look on his face. After a long pause, Burke inched his face close to my ear.

"Maybe it was just the beginning of an elk bugle," he whispered. "Sometimes they start out awfully strange."

A second, identical howl scotched that notion. The call was insistent and eerie, and I realized that my mouth was bone dry. There was another empty space, then a third wailing cry. Every minute, resonant quaver of pitch was perfectly clear. I could imagine the posture of the wolf, and the subtle motions of its upturned snout. I looked around at the bright blue sky, wondering if it could really be the middle of the day.

A light breeze rustled through the timber below, punctuated by squeaks from the fading chickadee flock. Finally Burke nudged my shoulder, and tentatively we edged forward to have a look at the lay of the terrain. We eased past a willow grove and sat down on an outcrop of brown shale, listening for the ticks of sharp claws against rocks. Burke withdrew an elk bugle from his pack and tooted a bit, but he never came near the quality of that yowl. The woods below our vantage point consisted of thick spruce and hemlock; it would be impossible to spot an animal on the ground. There was no use in fighting down the slope to search for sign, because we couldn't agree on the exact location of the howls. Close, certainly—within a hundred yards was our mutual guess. But we kept pointing at different spots on the mountainside, and if the wolf was still around we didn't want to disturb it by flailing through the brush.

Our whispers rose in volume until we were talking openly about where the wolf was, why it had been baying at midday, and whether the animal knew that two marmot-tracking humans were on the trail above it. We picked idly at the brilliant orange lichens crusted on the rocks, speculating on our chances of intercepting it again. No more signals rose from the woods below.

I expected any day with Tom Burke to hold an array of small pleasures, hidden details to learn about and treasure. This, however, was an event on a much larger scale, and the power of the howls had driven any thoughts of snails or marmots from our minds. Over the rest of lunch, we compared everything the two of us knew about wolves.

That wasn't a whole lot. Just how common the animals once were in this part of the country is not clear, because there is so little concrete evidence. Native tribes tell surprisingly few stories about them. The first written records for the Inland Northwest appear in journals of the explorer David Thompson, who on several occasions in the early 1800s found dead mule deer that had been run down and partially eaten by wolves. Diaries of other early visitors mention howls in the night and wolves attacking their horses. I told Burke about one account I had read, written by a trader who, walking alone near the Spokane River, was stopped in his tracks by what he described as an "immense" wolf with bared teeth.

"That's a good story," he agreed. "But it's just anecdotal evidence. And guess what? A hundred and fifty years later, that's still about all we've got."

He described a recent two-page listing of possible wolf sightings within the state from the previous three decades. Several of the reports came from northeastern Washington, and Burke had interviewed some of the people who made them. I pressed him for details: descriptions, track casts, scat samples. He looked at me as if I were dreaming.

"It's not that easy. When people see a big animal flash through the woods, 'grizzly' or 'wolf' snaps into their heads, and they're sure that's what they saw. Then some government agent like me shows up on their front porch and tries to hold a rational discussion. You should hear the sputtering: *'I guess I know a wolf when I see one!'*

"Of course, one thing that makes wolves so hard is that there's so many big dogs and crossbreeds out there, and the chances of seeing a real wolf are so slim. You've got to remember that these animals had a price on their heads for a long time."

Wolf pelts were still being traded at Fort Colville in the 1840s, when new settlers and missionaries began putting out strychnine to protect their cattle and horses. From then on everyone was after them, hunting and trapping. For a good portion of this century one of the Game Department's main jobs was to lace horse carcasses with poison to control predators. In addition, the state offered a cash bounty on wolves until the 1960s. Better than a century of such concentrated killing effectively wiped out wolf populations all across the West. A pair of confirmed wolves were poisoned on a carcass in the Okanogan in the 1890s, but after that verifiable reports are so scarce that taxonomists don't even know whether the original wolves that lived in the region belonged to the Rocky Mountain or the British Columbia subspecies.

"A trapper named Maynard ran some lines in the drainages below this ridge in the 1930s," Burke recounted. "He told us he never saw any evidence of a wolf pack even then, just a pair of big tracks that appeared every month or so. He figured it was a couple of young males slipping down from their home range up in Canada. Maynard said he never heard a howl the whole time he was here, and that man knows how to listen. One animal—one—trapped over in Tonasket in 1950 is the only sure wolf record for eastern Washington in the last fifty years."

Burke and I chewed our sandwiches and mulled over the situation, but we were too antsy to sit for very long. We stood up, stiff and shaky, and managed to travel another mile or two up the trail before turning around and marching right back to the brown outcrop. We sat there for another half hour with our ears pricked, scraping at the orange lichens. As the time ticked by, our degree of certainty as to exactly what we had heard began to waver.

"But what else could it have been?" asked Burke. "It wasn't a coyote, and we're awfully high up to run across a stray dog. On the one hand, a wolf sure seems like a long shot. On the other, some of the best reports on that list I was telling you about come from a ranch right below us, down on Slate Creek. The family there had sightings all through the sixties, and they sure sounded like they knew what they were talking about."

Burke stood up to stretch and looked north. A couple of peaks that straddled the Canadian border had recently been whitened by the first snowfall of the season.

"I went to hear this biologist from the University of Montana a couple of months ago, Bob Ream. He's been look-ing for sign in Glacier Park for a while now and has a system for telling the difference between wolf and dog tracks. He thinks some wolves are coming down from British Columbia, and that they might establish themselves in the park and then disperse from there. I wonder though, even if Ream's right, how it will all pan out. People and wolves haven't gotten along too well in the past."

Bob Ream squatted in a snowy field beside the North Fork of the Flathead River and carefully loaded his gear—picnic lunch, boots, collecting bags, radio receiver, antenna, poncho—into a huge Duluth pack, then slipped his cross-country skis into the side sleeves. Slabs of thick ice were stacked along the river's shore, and cold February nights had kept the river low enough to wade across into Glacier National Park. Surrounded by doghair stands of lodgepole pine and fine lumpy meadows, the North Fork here recalled other medium-sized river basins in the Inland Northwest. But this drainage was different, I kept telling myself: this one harbored wolves.

With packs bulging off our backs and waders pulled up tight around our bellies, Ream and I set off across the ford. The water was hypnotically clear, and the current fast enough to pluck rocks from the bottom and roll them downstream in loopy circles. I turned my face upstream and thought about each step very carefully. Ream strolled ahead, up to his waist in the frigid torrent, and could have forded the span twice in the time it took me to get across.

After hauling out on a gravel bar that had been the scene of a wolf kill only a few weeks before, we settled down to lunch behind a fractured ice floe. There had been three different kills near this spot, Ream said, the usual white-tailed deer and elk. When I asked if he'd found evidence of wolves eating anything else, he laughed and told me about another feeding site near Kintla Lake. Scattered among the bloodspots and small bits of fur were the feathers of an entire raven. That took me by surprise, and I wondered how a group of wolves could possibly sneak up on a raven, or why they would ever want to.

"I don't know," he replied dryly. "They must have been raven-ous."

Bob Ream's whimsy is matched by his patience, and since 1969 he has applied both of these virtues to the study of wolves. As a graduate student in Minnesota, he studied timber wolves for several years in the flat, wet, thickly wooded landscape of the Boundary Waters. In 1973, as a professor at the University of Montana, he founded the Wolf Ecology Project to see what could be learned about the uncertain status of wolves in the northern Rockies. Beginning with a scattering of reports about possible tracks and howls, and with a handful of stuffed specimens and moth-eaten hides, he mobilized a team of researchers to investigate leads on both sides of the Continental Divide. After five years his team had verified about four hundred different wolf sightings.

When a bear biologist working along the North Fork of the Flathead spotted a black-colored wolf in 1978, Ream had the permits to set a trap in the area. His researchers captured a light gray female just across the Canadian border, proving for the first time that there was anything besides wandering males in the drainage. After fitting the she-wolf with a radio collar and naming her Kishnena, they anxiously tracked her movements for the next sixteen months. But Kishnena only rarely entered the United States, and no other wolf tracks were found in association with hers.

"We had one animal," mused Ream as he finished his apple. "Since she traveled alone, most people assumed that she was past breeding age, and she spent almost all of her time north of the border. No one thought she was news."

Then in February of 1982, a biologist found a much larger track in step with Kishnena's, a distinct print with one toe missing. There was spotting on the snow, indicating that the female was in heat. That summer a park ranger drove up on seven wolf pups playing in the middle of a clearing only a few miles north of the international boundary. Almost a decade after the Wolf Ecology Project was formed, Ream had a group of wolves inside his study area.

While my hip waders slowly froze to the gravel bar, I learned that Kishnena disappeared after whelping that first litter, and for the next two summers there were no positive reports of new pups along the North Fork. Radio-collared members of her pack made only sporadic appearances in the area. Government funding tightened, and the pace of logging and oil exploration intensified on the British Columbia side of the border. At least two wolves were shot dead in the basin.

But some of Kishnena's pups held on to reach maturity, and in June of 1985, the wolf researchers made an aerial sighting of a female with seven all-black pups. Later that summer, researchers collared the mother, named Phyllis, and one of her female pups, named Kay. During the fall, the two spent most of their time south of the border along with ten other wolves. Now, as February sped into March, the pack was still around. Ream and his workers were in a state of constant alert: as long as good snow for tracking lasted, they would follow the animals. This might be the year that one of the females located her den—the first verified den in several decades—in the western United States.

Ream dug into his pack for the radio gear, unfolding his spindly antenna and standing up to strike a characteristic Statue of Liberty pose. There were three frequencies to listen for on his receiver: one set on a wandering male, another for Phyllis, the breeding female of the pack, and a third for her daughter Kay. When Ream turned the dial to Kay's number, faint beeps begin to knock on our ears.

"We're lucky today," he whispered, after comparing Kay's location with points on his map. "They're still in the same place as last night—must be on a kill."

This meant we could backtrack along their path from the previous day, looking for physical evidence of their movements, without worrying about harassing them. We reshouldered our packs and bushwhacked across a dry oxbow of river, where the low ground rose and fell in swaley bumps and was covered with a mixture of Englemann spruce and big cottonwoods. Our skis caught in the prickly spruce branches, but Ream moved steadily along, unperturbed, talking about wolves.

"Did you know that they still have wolves in India, in the Punjab? I just heard a story about an animal that came out of the forest in broad daylight and snatched a farmworker's infant from the edge of a field. And in Italy's Apennine Mountains there's a little wolf that sneaks down from the hills at night to scavenge for garbage with the village dogs. Hard to believe isn't it? Little trash dogs?"

We puffed up a shaley slope and met a primitive road that still retained a fair amount of snow among the windfall trees. After Bob unfolded his antenna to make sure the pack was still south of us, we strapped on our skis and whished slowly off in the opposite direction. Within half a mile we cut a series of tracks, one of them almost as big as my hand. Bob knelt down and framed the indentation with the spread of his arms.

"The track of a wolf." he announced. "How's it look to you?"

I sank to my haunches to study the pawmark. Its central pad was cut like a well-shaped keystone, and the four toes, each the size of my thumbprint, were flecked with the line of a long claw. In the crisp snow we could see feathered fur marks around the print, and follow the loping stride forward to the next set. We traced their course through the trees, where another set joined in, then another.

We followed the tracks until they disappeared into an impenetrable thicket of lodgepole, then returned to the road and headed north again. As the day began to wane with no more indications of wolf, we skied back to our point of entry, repacked our gear, and repeated the sticky bushwhack through the spruce bog. In late afternoon the bog was a maze of varied thrush song and elk tramples, but no wolf prints.

Finally the North Fork rose like thunder before us again. As I stood by the water, Ream tugged on his bibbed waders and restuffed his skis, all the while enumerating the various animal signs we had seen during the day. Moose. Elk. A mule deer traveling along a low ridge. Plenty of whitetail, and one huge beaver lodge.

"And hey! Did I tell you there've been some seals sighted up here, too?" He flopped down onto his belly, backpack and all, and rode an ice floe down to the river's edge, barking like a sea lion.

Two miles down the road, we set up the receiver again in the fading light. This time Kay's signal seemed to be very close, possibly in a opening just on the other side of the river. Ream stopped at a convenient finger of trees that jutted close to shore and quietly worked his way out to the edge. He drew in a deep breath, curled both hands around his mouth as if he might be cold, then suddenly cut loose with an inhuman shout so loud that I jumped back, startled in the same way I had been startled that day when I stood on Crowell Ridge. Ream's wrenching, soulful call carried on for long seconds before it cracked and slowly faded away.

A pair of animals answered him from downstream, a single pitch that split and grew until they become a chorus. Their initial response was followed by a single low moan from farther up the basin. Then the two groups caught onto each other, crying back and forth excitedly with the rich, expressive language of their kind, and the music rolled through the canopy of lodgepoles like a distant crowning fire. There were wolves out there, and they were wandering far across the land.

CLOUDBURST

*T*HE MORNING OF MAY 18 DAWNED clear, and a rush of birdsong pulled me out early to see what was about. When I discovered that a lazuli bunting had arrived from the south to assume its familiar perch on the powerline over Lynn Walker's greening alfalfa, I walked on down into the valley on the off chance that the local bobolinks had returned a few days early from their wintering grounds. Just as I reached the flatlands, a tremendous sonic boom scattered blackbirds and meadowlarks out of the timothy grass. I searched both for bobolinks and the source of such a powerful noise, but the birds in the field all looked dark to me, and there was no trace of a jet trail anywhere in the sky.

By the time I got back home, the Sunday sun had risen high. An hour after lunch I was curled up in the pinegrass beside the garden, dreaming of someplace else. When I woke up, it was a different day. Black storm clouds boiled over the horizon, and the fresh air of the morning had turned oppressively still. In need of refreshment, I struck out for a swimming hole in the creek below the house. The peculiar sky spread yellow-black colors along the trail, reminding me of hurricane days in the Southeast. As I descended into the canyon of Chewelah Creek, the clouds grew even darker, and it looked like we were in for our first heavy thunderstorm of the year.

In the intense humidity the swimming hole was inviting, but I decided to give the thunderhead a chance to pass over. Crossing the water on a fallen log, I followed a set of stone steps up the opposite bank to the front door of Babe Reynolds's shop. The building was open but empty, dark and cool inside. In the middle of the floor sat a cupboard of clear white pine, recently glued and clamped in Babe's meticulous style. Zero tolerance. I circled the cupboard, feeling its curlicues and tight joints with my fingers, before stepping back outside. The luxurious plant growth of May filled the languid air with pungent smells.

A low rumble of thunder sounded on the periphery of my hearing as I paced around to the back porch. Before I could raise my hand to knock, two small dogs were yapping at the sliding glass door. Trying unsuccessfully to quiet her toy poodles, Mike ushered me into the living room, where Babe lay floating in his black recliner in front of the television. Clad only in boxer shorts, he was watching John Wayne direct the U.S. Cavalry in an old western. Mike apologized for Babe's lack of attire while she folded laundry on a chair.

"Honey, these pants are still wet. Why'd you take them out of the dryer so soon?"

Babe ignored his wife's complaints and ratcheted his LazyBoy upright.

"Did you hear?" he asked softly. "She blew up this morning."

I was about to ask who he meant when, as if on cue, tiny letters crawled across the bottom of the John Wayne movie to announce a complete volcano update at six p.m. The words were replaced by images of an undulating, smoky mass, and Babe leaned forward to cheer.

"Look at that baby! Blow, you mountain. *Blow!*"

"Oh, Babo," said Mike.

Now I understood what had happened—Mount St. Helens, near Portland, had been puffing out smoke and ash all spring. Now it had finally erupted. It was a true geological event, and Babe knew we were witnessing destiny.

"Eight-oh-two this morning," he said. "Took the whole top of the mountain off."

I remembered the sonic boom that had scattered the blackbirds. That had been right around eight o'clock, but it was hard to believe I could have heard the actual eruption— Mount St. Helens was over two hundred miles away.

"And old Harry Truman," Babe continued. "They don't know yet what in the hell happened to him." He collapsed back into his chair with a look of sadness. "And those people in the campground. I wish they hadn't had to die. I hate to see people die."

Babe had been watching the news all afternoon and filled me in on everything he knew about the day's events. He waved his arms aloft to describe the unimaginable heat waves rolling down off Mount St. Helens, and the shower of exploded rocks that covered the sky.

"If only Harry would have come down off that mountain," Mike fretted. "Why wouldn't he just leave when he had the chance?"

The volcano disappeared from the TV screen, and Babe hushed us as a group of bluebellies crooned around a very young John Wayne.

"Shut up," Babe ordered. "Just calm down for a minute. Listen to this." He cocked his ear to the screen and lifted his chin to the ceiling, following the complex chord changes and tight harmonies of the love song.

"Music," he said. "This is *music*."

When John Wayne got his wagons rolling again, Babe followed him, spinning out a narrative about his own family's migration west from Indiana. In 1902 his parents set out for California with all their belongings and Babe's aged grandmother in a single wagon. They had pushed as far as Tucumcari, New Mexico, when the old lady died. Babe's mother went to pieces, forcing their return to the Midwest. Four years later the folks set out again in the same covered wagon. They had almost made it to the Sacramento Valley when a new volcano update ran across the bottom of the TV screen. This one ended with a shot of a river choked with logs and running fast, wreaking destruction on an incomprehensible scale.

"This is too much," Babe said. "To get to see something like this in our lifetime—it's just miraculous."

The river scene vanished, and Babe's attention returned to John Wayne and his party, running for the rocks before an endless wave of advancing Apaches. Several amazing horse stunts and one disintegrating wagon raced past before the whites reached a sheltered outcrop and began to pick off the Indians one by screaming one. As John Wayne promised the woman clinging to his arm that if they ever got out of this jam he would buy a farm and settle down, Babe broke in.

"Just like Dad. Nothing ever came easy for him, but he finally scraped together a ranch in the Sacramento Delta. It was a wide open place for us kids, even if it never was worth much. I can remember tramping around in the marsh with a little .22, scared to shoot at anything 'cause I might waste the bullet. We learned to look for food that didn't need shooting.

Tugboats used to push barges full of asparagus down the river, and we'd paddle out into the water to pick up the stalks that floated loose. Good old asparagus.

"One day my father told me that his friend Louie Frias was coming from Indiana with his famous draft horses. I was out of the house right after supper, staring down our road for the Frias caravan. It was a long, straight road, and you could see for miles. I stood out there watching that empty road for weeks, until finally one evening I saw a dust cloud way off in the distance. Then up came a team of thirty horses pulling one huge wagon, big bastard workhorses, and Louie Frias in command, yelling and cursing something fierce. He had a long black bull whip that he'd snake out and crack right on their necks. Louie was a little runt of a man, and he was treating those horses terrible. There was no way I could like him after that."

A new set of letters crawled beneath the movie, this time warning of an ash cloud headed east.

"What?" Mike asked. "That volcano is coming here? To us?"

I looked at Babe as if he had been holding something back. Mike and I rushed to the windows, squinting past the canyon slopes to inspect the progress of the looming thunderstorm. The clouds didn't look like any weather I had ever seen before. We turned back to the television as a reporter's head filled the screen, an uncertain expression on his face. He spoke to someone off camera before carefully starting to read in his most professional voice.

"The U.S. Weather Bureau and the Washington State Patrol report that the ash cloud from Mount St. Helens is moving in an easterly direction at approximately fifteen miles per hour. Several inches of ash have already fallen around the Ritzville area, and Interstate 90 is now closed west of Spokane. Spokane area residents are advised to return to their homes as soon as possible. Officials caution that the ash

may be harmful if inhaled. If you find it necessary to be out-
doors, they recommend that you cover your mouth and nose
with a damp cloth."

The broadcast cut to an interview with a deputy sheriff
who was not so composed.

"Don't drive anywhere," sputtered the officer. "This ash'll
ruin your motor. All our patrol units in Ritzville are down
already, and we have no idea how many cars are stranded on
the highway. We've also had word that some of the elements
in this ash may react with water. Do not, under any circum-
stances, breathe through a wet cloth. Get inside and close all
your windows and doors tight. Tune to the emergency frequency of your radio for further updates."

It sounded like time to head for home. Saying my good-
byes, I stepped outside into a gritty haze that draped the
afternoon in tones of gray. White dust settled quietly on the
new green growth beside the creek, and as I crossed the log
bridge I watched an ashy film gather on the surface of a still
pool. It was a grit I could taste, not sandy or chalky, but sharp
as ground glass. By the time I ascended the slope on the far
side of the canyon, I was running to get inside my house.

The morning after the eruption, no birds sang. I wondered what it must be like for those bobolinks, completing
their long flight up from the tropics, to flap directly into a
rolling cloud of silica dust. The path of the volcanic ash
cloud passed just to the south of Stevens County, so that our
accumulation amounted to only about an eighth of an inch.
From the news reports it was obvious that towns down in
the Columbia Basin were in much worse shape, but during
the general bewilderment of the first forty-eight hours, it
was difficult to tell exactly what constituted a disaster. While

the most lurid rumors about the stuff turned out to be false, the ash did creep through every crack in the house, coating floors and dishes with a caustic dust. Repeated vacuumings left behind as much as they sucked up, and each time a door opened, more ash swirled inside. I didn't even consider driving but did scratch the paint on my pickup by carefully sweeping the hood clean with a push broom.

Then it began to rain. Storms pushed across the Cascades for two weeks without a break, washing away much of the ash. In Stevens County we were able to enjoy the delightful terror of that first black afternoon, participate for a couple more days in the general panic generated northward from Ritzville and Spokane, and then pretty much resume life as normal. Many gutters came down from the weight of their ash loads. Several farmers damaged haying equipment by exposing moving steel parts to endless rounds in the grit. Some people spent the whole summer with their faces hidden behind dust masks. But by the end of May, male bobolinks were performing their aerial displays over the fields at the bottom of our hill, and I decided that we had escaped the effects of any real cataclysm. The mountain continued to belch and puff at irregular intervals, and the citizens down-wind were kept on constant alert as to the dangers that might lie ahead. You could never tell, the media kept saying. The next one might be worse.

Certainly this part of the country had seen much worse. Any visible roadcut revealed ash layers, some of them several inches thick, from volcanic episodes that dated back thousands of years. People of the Spokane tribe told early white visitors in the 1840s about an event within their memory, a long night filled with terrible thunder. Their hearts grew small, they said, and they feared the world would fall to pieces. The Spokane chief known as Cornelius remembered awakening in his lodge as a boy to the sound of thunder and people crying out in terror. When he ran outside, he thought at first that it was snowing, then realized that dirt was falling from the sky.

Two months after Mount St. Helens' big eruption, I started a landscaping job just south of Spokane. The house sat on the edge of the channeled scablands that had been scoured and carved as the bursting floods of glacial Lake Missoula tore through the Columbia Basin, and an ocean of scaly, loose basalt surrounded the site—material well suited for flatrock walkways and garden retaining walls. This area had been directly in the path of the St. Helens blast, however, and everything was iced with ash a half-inch thick. The recent rains had only succeeded in gluing the ash particles together into a gummy white paste. When I rolled over the first stone, a puff of fine gray-white dust wafted straight into my face. I retreated to my truck and dug a dust mask out of the glovebox. The filter made my work that much more sweaty, and as I flopped the rocks around through the day, odd questions kept coming into my mind. What did people do with their dogs in this stuff? How could plants grow or snakes crawl? What did the bottoms of ponds and streambeds look like around here? How many years would it take for the ash to be completely absorbed?

It wasn't long before I was covered with it. Rivulets of sweat cut channels through a tawny coating on my forearms and face, and drops fell from my body onto the fractured rock, itself once part of an enormous magma flow. Dying for a drink of water, I cracked open the door of the house. The owner's wife looked up from her reading chair as a gray cloud drifted in from the searing desert. Ash settled down on the lime green rug in her den, and her expression of greeting melted, then changed to one of genuine concern.

"Haven't you heard?" she asked. "Mount St. Helens has blown off again. They say it's headed this way, maybe a little farther north this time. That would be fine with me—I've had just about enough of this."

North meant home. I gently backed out the door, raising another spore cloud of dust. Motoring toward Chewelah on Highway 395, I listened to the mayor of Spokane on the radio. Eruption number four had been a fairly large one, with an ash plume that reached forty-seven thousand feet into the atmosphere. Its pathway seemed to be a little north of previous ones. Word was coming in of fallout to the south and west, north through the Okanogan Valley, and as far east as the Idaho panhandle. Wait a minute, Mayor, I wanted to say. Surely ash can't be falling in all those places at once. At the stoplight in Chewelah, I decided to climb the hill up by the airport, which offered a good long view to the west, and see what I could see.

As I approached my turnout, I came upon Babe Reynolds's pink Army surplus Jeep sideways on the shoulder of the road. The Jeep's front end had sunk into loose sand, while the rear lay pretty far down in the ditch. Babe was still behind the wheel and didn't seem all that pleased to see me.

"Well, Jesus Christ," he snarled when I stopped. "How am I going get out of here and downtown by five o'clock?"

When I suggested that he wasn't going to make it by closing time, he grunted without stirring from his seat. I dug a chain out of my truck and was turning to hook it up when a glance to the southwest revealed a brilliant sunset of hazy oranges. Far away the basin scablands were fading slowly beneath a perfectly clear sky. Venus glowed in that indigo space, minutes ahead of the fainter stars. Then Babe directed my gaze a quarter-turn to the northwest.

There a dark force crept along the horizon, as frills of the deepest black curled up to merge with the indigo. It was a

look of midnight, long before midnight was due. The blackness collected itself into the shape of a colossal human torso,
a giant Goya painting that hovered over the north country.
The giant's black shoulder dipped and turned, and the gray
dust rained down once more. I could visualize blooming mariposa lilies, recently emerged in the summer's heat, accepting
a taste of fine ash. Machines left out in the yard passed
through my mind, and then I remembered that it had been so
pleasant when I departed for work that morning that I left all
my windows wide open. Soon they would be welcoming a
new ashfall straight into the house. I started to move, but
Babe's thick arm curled out from the window of the Jeep to
grab my shoulder.

"Wait just a minute," he said, with a serenity that brought
a bloom to his whole face. "We'll never see anything like this
again in our whole lives."

I licked the gritty dryness from my lips. The colossus
bowed lower, pouring his dust, then turned and blended
slowly with the darker skies to the east. Babe smiled at his
departure. We watched until night and its proper stars spread
across the rest of the sky, then started looking for a flashlight
so we could hook up the tow chain.

LISTENING

"WE AGREED THIS WAY WAS better than traps," said Bev Drake as we paced around her garden plot. "I mean, don't you think it's fair to attack them straight on when they're tearing up your crop? When you use a trap, aren't you just transporting the problem to somewhere else?"

Bev lived on a reclaimed homestead on Stranger Creek, high in the Huckleberry Range, and she and her family liked to solve their problems right there. Their nemesis this spring was porcupines in the strawberry patch. Their solution at first was simply to trap the spiny creatures and remove them, but for the past week, just as the young berries were starting to come on, the porcupines had been winning the battle. Bev had set up a watch the night before to confront the animals, stationing herself between the rows with a firewood-splitting

ax in hand. She hadn't been there long when a porcupine
waddled out of the woods.

"As soon as it saw me it prickled up those quills, and I
couldn't tell where to hit the thing. There's this pea head,
tucked in the middle of a pincushion, and no place to aim. I
tried to shoo it away with the flat of the ax, but it wasn't
going anywhere. Then it nosed right into a strawberry bush
and started eating! I raised the ax to whack it, but . . . oh,
what's a few strawberries?"

We were above the garden now, beginning a walk from
Stranger Creek over to the Columbia River. The morning air
at this elevation still clutched the previous night's chill. Bev
rubbed her sleepy eyes as we passed through a lush growth of
grand firs, and it wasn't long before the fluted notes of a
Swainson's thrush spilled through the canopy.

"Hear that?" I turned one ear in its direction. "That's a
good one."

Bev liked to learn a bird song once in a while. She was a
speech therapist, and listening formed an integral part of her
work. For years she had carried her hearing-test kit around to
the elementary schools in northern Stevens County, hooking
kids up to the earphones and recording the cycles at which
they lost the high- and low-pitched tones on her tape. Her
method of winning the confidence of high-school boys was to
predict before she handed them the phones that they would
be deaf in their right ears, and enough of them hunted with
deer rifles that she was usually right.

My first meeting with Bev had been several years before,
when a mutual friend asked me to deliver a message to the
local Head Start Program. The classes took place inside the
original town bank, a thick square building as solid as a rock.
On my way down the central hallway, I heard what sounded
like muffled groans escaping from the old vault. Concerned,
I approached the vault and peeked around its heavy steel

door. There was Bev Drake, her back to me, bending intently toward a little boy. A cascade of sounds spilled from her mouth: "UUUUU EEEEE EEEEEUUUUU OOOOOOOOOO HU HU HU UH O! O! O! AHH AHHH AHHHHHHHH . . ." She enthusiastically encouraged the boy to repeat, to say clearly, to project.

Bev's pupil, perhaps eight years old, remained completely focused on her face, imitating the muscles of her mouth. His lips and tongue wobbled elastically. He wrapped his mouth around a large O and tongued it back, filling the vault with the long vowel. When Bev stopped the drill and clapped him hard on his back, the boy burst into raucous laughter. Bev joined him for a moment, then started back in again on his UUUUUUs and EEEEEEs.

The Swainson's thrush was quite close now. It rolled out another ascending chorus and faded into the background of dark green foliage.

"How does it do that?" asked Bev. "I can hear two or three strands of the same thread."

She whistled to herself, trying to imitate the flutelike thrush notes as we continued up the creek past a series of beaver dams. Water poured through each mishmash of loose sticks and limbs, but the dams still held back enough of the creek to form a chain of separate ponds. The largest one was crisscrossed with downed birches and cottonwoods. All along the shore we found fresh chew marks and the paths of dragged alder limbs. A male wood duck jumped up from a protected cove and shot away with startled whistles, and the song of another Swainson's thrush echoed behind it.

Above the ponds some of the trees were marked with the painted orange rings of an impending logging job, and I remembered that a big timber company owned a lot of land above Bev's meadow.

"Next spring," she said. "Not this year, but the next, that's when we're on their schedule. We've been talking to the cruiser when he comes in, to find out how they're going to do it."

It was an interesting piece of forest. All kinds of coniferous species flourished on the extra moisture of the north slope, from Douglas fir and grand fir to hemlock and spruce. Their new spring growth produced an abstract patchwork of colors and shapes that blanketed the hillside. Yet none of the trees were particularly old, and the road we walked on was undoubtedly a former trunk road for gathering logs.

"We can stand the logging," Bev went on. "We knew who owned this land when we bought our place. But we're a little concerned about which trees they decide to cut. Come look at these."

She cut off the dirt road and followed an animal trail toward a distinct rocky-topped knob. At its base we entered a stand of huge tamaracks tucked neatly against the slope, so that a person walking on the road could easily have missed them. It was an eerie group of trees, packed so close together that I couldn't walk between some of them. Their butts were four or more feet in diameter and rose up clear for several log lengths before the first fat, contorted branches made their appearance. Bark flaked off in shades of deep pinks and oranges, not the paler buckskin of dying trees. Within the grove a dense carpet of yellow needles completely muffled our footsteps.

"The cruiser said they must be really old," Bev said. "At this elevation, in this dry climate, with this rocky soil, he guessed it might take two or three hundred years for a group of trees to grow this tall. We call them the Virgins, and we're trying to negotiate with the company to leave them alone.

They say fine, as long as we buy every board foot of what's left standing. Want to make a donation?"

From the Virgins, we stepped up our pace for a few miles, until we broke over the divide between the Colville and Columbia drainages. After that, the land dried out into open slopes dappled by the broad woolly leaves of bloomed-out balsamroot sunflowers. The hillside crackled with the desiccated clicks of grasshoppers, and a late-singing sparrow trilled out its buzzy song. Through the midday haze, we soon began to get views of the Columbia River, although no one who lives here calls it the Columbia anymore: it's Lake Roosevelt, "The Lake," a hundred miles of slack water backed up behind Grand Coulee Dam. Before us spread a wide vista: north to the orchards below Kettle Falls, west across the water to the open pine hills of the Colville Reservation, south to the land of the Spokane tribe.

Bev listened to the sparrow songs, nodding, then began to tell me about a new client on the Spokane Reservation. She was an older woman, a stroke victim. Since coming home from the hospital, the lady only sat in her chair and stared. Apparently she couldn't speak at all anymore, but it was not clear whether the problem was with her muscles or her memory. Two of her children, hoping to reteach their mother to talk, got in touch with Bev.

For the past several weeks Bev had carried on sessions with the woman, trying to get her to repeat basic vowel and consonant sounds. This method had worked to varying degrees with other stroke patients, but this woman was older, and did not seem to be responding. During the first three visits she simply continued to stare, and everyone grew discouraged. On the fourth week she began vocalizing back at Bev, but the sounds were strange. Bev kept pointing to the tip of her tongue and the front roof of her mouth, showing the exact touch of her lips as they produced a sound—that was the way she taught the mechanics of speech. But her patient made noises that originated clear down at the root of her tongue, noises that did not fall within Bev's normal range of speech.

After several frustrating sessions Bev finally had a stroke of illumination: the lady was forming the basic sounds of a completely different language. A few questions to the family revealed that the woman had learned her native Spokane first as a child, then forgotten it at the missionary school—no "Indian talk" was allowed there. She spoke only English for several decades, until the disruption caused by the stroke started her over again in her native tongue.

"I guess I should let her go," Bev said. "There's really not much I can do. The family is teaching her themselves now. One of the uncles has the language, and he is very patient. But I'm curious to see where she ends up."

She fingered the bottom of her chin while she moved muscles inside her throat. She swallowed, and caught the gulp like a frog. From somewhere between her teeth she creaked like a chewing insect.

The missionary Elkanah Walker spent much of the 1840s trying to convert bands of Spokane, Kalispel, and Colville people to Christianity. He was frustrated by many obstacles, but none more than language. Walker undertook to assemble the first written alphabet of the Spokane tongue and in 1839 wrote a letter to a colleague describing his work.

> As respects my progress in the language, it is quite slow. This ought to be expected as I have had so much labor to perform & the want of a good teacher. The Old Chief would be a good teacher were he not so old. His teeth are almost gone & his pronunciation is very bad . . . we have not yet formed an alphabet.

"Maybe that's what I need," remarked Bev. "A few more teeth in my mouth."

We sat for a few minutes longer, watching a field of luxurious pink vetch wave in the air. Then we got up and walked, all downhill now, intent on wetting our feet in the big river. It meant a couple more hours of hiking, through land studded with wild outcrops of pillow basalt and runaway stones. Bev, in a tone of hushed sympathy, told me that the annual precipitation here was pegged at around twelve inches total of rain and snow.

From our vantage on the hillside, we had a clear view upstream to the route of a ferry as it worked its way back and forth across the river, from the settlement of Gifford to the Colville Indian Reservation. Each trip took about twenty minutes, and we watched as the diesel-powered barge received three or four cars, snuggled them into position, then pushed off from shore upstream. Halfway across, the current would float the ferry back down along a parabolic arc, landing it at a dusty concrete pad below the town of Inchelium.

The road we walked hit the river highway a couple of miles downstream from the ferry. Our legs ached pleasantly on the hard asphalt as we started the trek up to Gifford, where we had arranged to rendezvous with a car. Irrigation pumps made water available for crops, and before too long we passed a beautiful patch of sweet corn covering an acre or more. Already knee-high and thickly green, it was fine looking corn; not only had Lake Roosevelt provided the water, but its thermal mass had gained the farmer at least a month over Bev's strawberry patch on the other side of the ridge.

A red mailbox marked the start of a dirt driveway, at the end of which we could see a little frame house tucked against a basalt escarpment. As Bev leaned against the mailbox, taking a drink of water from her canteen, a screen door slammed and two small children made their way down the

driveway toward us. The one in front, a boy right at the edge
of school age, was grasping what looked like a piece of rubber
hose in each hand. As he neared the mailbox, we saw that the
twin appendages were actually a pair of stubby dead rattle-
snakes. His dad had surprised them out in the corn patch a few
hours before, the boy announced, and showed us how the
larger one carried seven buttons at the end of its tail, the
smaller five.

When his little sister caught up, she helped her brother
put the serpents through a ritual display. They laid the stout
bodies on the ground and invited Bev and me to squat down
and trace their shapes and contours. With the children's
encouragement, we stroked the rough diamond scales on the
fat backs and let the shivers run down our spines. We fingered
the chitinous kernels behind one snake's tail, noting how
each husk beautifully tapered down to the next button.

I was starting to wonder about the longevity of snake
venom when Bev blurted out, "Does your mom know you're
out here playing with these things?"

"Sure," the boy answered, and the pair bent back to their
work. With supple fingers, they began to probe at the nostrils
and lips. The boy punched up the squat rhomboid head of his
serpent to show its heat-sensing pits and bulging eyes.

"Is this really a good idea?" Bev asked, her voice edging
toward concern. "Didn't Jim tell Huck Finn that no good
comes from handling snakeskins?"

I found two fruitwood sticks and tried to get the children
to use them as probes, but they tossed them aside. The boy
picked his snake up and shook its tail in my face, chattering
his teeth along with the rattles.

"Hear that?" he challenged. "Can't make that noise with
a stick."

Bev covered her ears, but the more we squirmed, the
more the little ones showed off. Their snakes were alive; they

were wonderful. The boy whipped his rattlesnake back into its place beside his sister's, then rubbed its nose in the dirt. He picked up the body again and pretended to take a bite out of it. He squeezed its cheeks, baring the curved ivory needles of the upper fangs. The black tendon of the tongue drooped out, forked and expressive, as if the snake were trying to speak.

DANCE

*T*HE FIRST TEN DAYS OF APRIL WERE AS
blustery and cold as a stretch of February. Our
driveway, which had recently given up the frost and
turned into a bottomless quagmire, refroze with the cracks
and pressure ridges of an alpine glacier. Yellow snow lilies that
had been poised to bloom abruptly disappeared. People
approaching each other downtown would cross the street
rather than listen to more complaints about the interminable
delays of spring. When state game biologist Steve Zender
asked me to join his annual count of sharp-tailed grouse sites
in the next county south, I jumped at the chance.

Though it was early afternoon when we left Chewelah,
the temperature had barely risen above the freezing mark,
and Steve had to slow for black ice on the highway. We
skirted the edge of the Spokane Reservation, watching the
terrain change from forested mountains to the spare land-

scape of mesa and coulee that marks the Columbia Basin. The mixture of coniferous trees dropped away, leaving only short, fat yellow pines spaced across the wide flats. Except for drifted gray clumps lurking in the shadows along northern exposures, the snow was all gone.

As we rode along, Steve filled me in on his latest doings. He had made a couple of day trips in search of some elusive introduced mountain goats, but couldn't tell yet how well they might be doing. There was a familiar controversy about whether to open an either-sex deer season in October, and Steve was caught in the middle of an argument between abundant animals and a shortage of good winter range. Over on the Pend Oreille River, a court case that he had hoped would end a cougar-poaching houndsman's career had resulted only in a light fine and a suspended sentence.

"After an afternoon on the witness stand," he said, "all I want to do is get out of this muck and walk around."

On the long descent to the Spokane River, the afternoon sun began to heat up the cab of the pickup. We turned west and rolled past a riot of ducks and shorebirds packed into a network of pothole marshes. It was as if we had just crossed a line between winter and spring, and all the migrant birds were entrenched on this side, waiting for the weather to break.

Soon we were surrounded by wheat farms, fields of brown fallow or green sprouts relieved only by an occasional shallow coulee or rough butte too rocky to cultivate. Around the rocks every untilled inch was carpeted with desert parsleys, spring beauties, wild onions, and sagebrush showing fresh growth. Steve rolled his window down to drink in the bracing new smells. Right beside us, a ferruginous hawk jumped off a fencepost and glided up a draw, its white tail ruffled around thick, tawny leggings.

This would be my third spring helping Steve with his grouse counts, and I was curious about how the familiar leks were doing. The range of the sharp-tailed grouse had been shrinking ever since wheat farming arrived in the region. The birds' spring gathering leks had been plowed up, and the aspen groves that they used for winter roosts and spring nourishment had been cut down. But lately some farmers had developed an appreciation for the grouse and were giving them more room. Steve said word had it that sharpies had been displaying full tilt at most of their known leks, and after we finished our census, he hoped to spend a little time searching for new sites.

The homogenous wheat fields faded into a patch of rocky, wild scablands, and we turned onto a track along a powerline right-of-way. A fresh breeze was beginning to pick up as the temperature dropped in the waning afternoon. Swirling volcanic ash muted the sun to pastel shades of orange, but it remained warm around the basalt columns that rimmed the coulee. We got out to explore a pothole lake surrounded by a healthy marsh, tracking the gabbles and quacks of ducks on the move. From high above the pond, the percussive music of sandhill cranes in flight rained down on us. By the time we got back to the pickup, we were ready to pack it in for the day.

At the end of the powerline road we found our campsite from the previous April. While we unloaded our gear, Steve pointed across a huge field of alfalfa to a two-story farmhouse, faded and alone in the midst of the open landscape.

"I hear we might have some company here this year," he commented. "There's a falconer living on that place now, and he must be a good one. Everybody in the Game Department's heard of him—a few years ago he got caught on the coast with some extra birds. Supposedly he's gone straight and says he wants to work with us, sort of as a promoter of clean falconry. I wonder why he chose a place like this?"

I thought of the variety of raptors that wintered here in the open desert, the abundance of horned larks, shorebirds, and ducks for prey, and the utter lack of disruptive humans.

"I sure can't think of a better place for the birds," I said. "Remember his name?"

"Kirk something, I think. Kirk Benedict. You don't know him, do you?"

It was that job in the scablands, the one that called for so much stonework. While I ran basalt kneewalls and stairways around a wide patio, two carpenters finished up the house; Kirk Benedict was the one who wore a gray alpaca cap and purple Guatemalan sweater vest. He was compactly built, and beneath the Andean cap his face was dark and crinkled from squinting into the sun. We were introduced to each other as sharing an interest in birds, and Kirk didn't waste a minute before asking if I knew of any merlin nests in the mountains north of Spokane. Miffed that anyone in a purple sweater vest would consider snooping around a merlin nest near the place where I lived, I grunted a tight "no" and went back to work. But Kirk turned out to be irresistible, following me around the house and spouting information about every kind of raptor, revealing a knowledge of those birds that far surpassed my own.

During the two weeks he remained on the job, he filled me in on his career. He had captured a great horned owl at the tender age of nine, and his secret training of the bird hooked him forever on the rituals of falconry. His life since then had repeated a constant run of search, trap, train, and throw, each short cycle broken off when the loss or purposeful release of a bird allowed him to begin anew.

"You've got to find them first," said Kirk. "There's not that many good places for a falcon to winter in this hemisphere, and a person can learn those, but you've got to be ready when one appears where you don't expect it. Catching them, that's the easy part—if you can tie knots and throw a pigeon, you can trap a falcon. Most of the time, that is. As soon as I get a new bird, I take it into a dark room right away, where it's completely quiet. I hold some fresh meat in my hand, and we sit there together until the bird eats it. Sometimes that takes a few days, till we're both about to starve. But if a falcon won't take the meat from me, things aren't going to work out. I've let a lot go free that wouldn't eat."

Plenty of adventures had grown out of Kirk's compulsion, and he loved to spin out the yarns. There was the January when he nearly froze to death trying to capture a stubborn gyrfalcon along the breaks of the Missouri River. During a nesting season in the Northwest Territories, he snatched a tundra peregrine chick from the middle of a prestigious academic study. Scanning from the top of a ruined pyramid in Oaxaca, he discovered a lost population of orange-breasted bat falcons but decided not to even try and capture one because they fit the place so well. Anything that sidetracked Kirk from his true calling he regarded as a humorous interlude, whether it involved dressing up in medieval costume to fly prairie falcons at a plush Mojave Desert dude ranch, or cooling off in a jail cell after the Game Department nailed him for noose-trapping in the Skagit River Delta.

No matter how far Kirk's escapades overstepped my own bird ethics, his single-minded reverence for falcons and the tradition of human falconry kept me listening. Kirk swore that he never took an egg that the female would not immediately replace, or a chick that would have survived the competition from its nest mates. Any wintering bird he trapped was left to fly free in the spring. He never used jesses, so that if he failed to catch up with his bird while it was feeding after a kill, it could simply fly away—no matter.

One afternoon we were watching a group of pygmy nuthatches swarm through a stand of yellow pines when the birds suddenly stopped feeding. They dove as a single unit for the closest solid trunk and clung to the bark, motionless. Kirk pointed quickly to a merlin that cut across the horizon, homed on the tree, and then darted away. He absorbed every move of raptor and prey during the few seconds that it took the scene to play out, and when the merlin disappeared and the nuthatches began to twitter again, Kirk smiled gaily.

"Those nuthatches are so quick. And they work together in the flock so well, it's a wonder any merlin can ever nab one. But, you know, some big birds can be just as crafty. I found that out working for Disney."

A wildlife film director had needed shots of a prairie falcon stooping on sharp-tailed grouse. Easy enough, said Kirk, and after thoroughly scouting the area, he set up several flights designed to please the cameraman. Yet even though each stoop looked letter-perfect from Kirk's vantage point on a ridge, the film crew insisted that the falcon never took a grouse. Kirk remained baffled until he watched the footage in slow motion.

As the camera rolled, the prairie falcon eased up on the hiding place of a sharp-tailed grouse. The grouse exploded from its cover with a burst of short-winged power that initially left the prairie falcon behind, but then the hunter closed in with deep, steady wingbeats. Within moments its talons were poised over the exhausted grouse's back. A strike seemed imminent, but at the last instant the grouse jerked its wings into its body, tucked like a gymnast, and plummeted to earth. With the prairie falcon diving to follow, the chunky grouse hit the ground in a cloud of dust and rolled wildly through the sage; it tumbled to a stop, then simply tipped up on its thick feet and disappeared into its natural cover. The prairie falcon continued to glide, pulling up when it lost the proper angle on the grouse. From a distance it looked like a sequence of stoop, impact, and kill, but absolutely no contact was made.

"That's a hunt," concluded Kirk, his eyes flashing with excitement. "That's a bird worth hunting."

Steve and I knew that early-morning lek surveys were always a test of endurance, so after supper we let the fire die away and unrolled our sleeping bags. But the spring excitement overrode our fatigue. We kept mumbling things under the stars, then watched the brilliant rise of a near-full moon. Thirty minutes later we were talking loudly and sitting up straight. What the heck, we decided—I might never run into Kirk Benedict again. A spring visit was really the neighborly thing to do.

We scrambled back into the pickup and bumped back down the right-of-way to the county road. In the distance I could see two yard lights twinkling from a pair of well-spaced ranches that ran cattle in the scablands. Kirk's older farmhouse stood completely separate from their world of feedlots and wheat, and Steve and I quit talking when we turned down the long track that led to his house. A few bare mountain ash trees bordered the driveway, their bark silver in the moonlight.

We sat in front of the weather-beaten clapboard house for several minutes without moving. A Volkswagen was in the driveway, and a bulb burned in the kitchen, but it's not always easy to pay a social call on a falconer in a Game Department pickup.

The back door opened, and a woman dressed in a wool skirt and man's work shirt stepped onto the porch. In a moment Steve and I were seated in the kitchen, blinking in the light as the lady introduced herself. Her name was Dianne. She was Kirk's girlfriend, but he was in Spokane and wouldn't return until Thursday.

Dianne seemed to have inherited a touch of homestead loneliness from whatever solitary heroine had lived in this house before, and she rattled on as if she had been without company for a solid winter instead of only two days. Steve encouraged her need to talk; when he mentioned sharp-tailed grouse, Dianne willingly pointed toward the leks and budding roosts that Kirk had under surveillance. Meanwhile, I was having trouble suppressing a terrible fear that Kirk himself was in the house. I could picture him crouched in a closet, muffling two hooded gyrfalcons and a crate of pheasant chicks. While Dianne chattered on, I scanned the disarray of clothes and tools in the room, wondering exactly what I would do if I saw anything suspicious.

Finally Steve caught my eye and indicated by a subtle jerk of his head that we should be leaving. Dianne accompanied us to our pickup, repeating how sorry Kirk would be to have missed us and inviting us to supper on Thursday night. Steve nodded, shook his head, nodded, and slowly eased back out the driveway.

"Whew," he whispered, when we were safely turned around. "That lady can talk."

This time we stayed in our bags, although sleep wasn't any nearer than before. Coot laughter from the pothole marsh mocked my attempts to get comfortable on the rocky ground, and nearby I could hear Steve thrashing around in much the same fashion. As the temperature beneath the waning moon fell below twenty degrees, short-eared owls boomed over us in sudden swoops.

Before Pacific Daylight Savings Time arrives in northeast Washington, April mornings start around three thirty a.m. Steve and I were both on our feet with the first gray light, puffing up and down the road to restart our frozen circulation. We listened for grouse sounds for several minutes in the half-dark, and caught faint hoots and flutters from across the field. Steve whipped out his metal clipboard to check off the first lek as "active." We saluted each other with a crust of the previous evening's bread and crept off in the icy pickup toward our next circle of dance.

We had checked off two more known active leks, without getting too close, when Steve pulled into a turnout a few miles from our campsite. We hopped a fence and made for gray farm buildings that stood ghostly in the new light, then stopped and turned around in the open sage, listening intently. The spot looked good, but there was no sign of any birds—no stamped-down bunchgrasses, not a single dropping, no distant drums.

"This way," Steve whispered, motioning.

I squatted and stared west across fenceposts and scattered sage. When the morning breeze quieted for a moment, I caught a slight movement along the line of vegetation. In the unsure dawn, it looked like the spread fingers of a waving hand. More hands appeared above the sagebrush. I thought I heard a distant tooting sound and realized that Steve, too, was hearing something. We paced forward as quickly as we could without tripping on the scaly rocks.

Soon the hands sharpened into fringed wingtips that floated up, then vanished into the olive gray brush. My ears picked out the sound of sturdy legs pounding the ground. We crossed a fence and crept up the lip of a slight rise.

On the far side of the hump, a shallow basin opened before us. There, in a bunchgrass-softened bowl, two dozen sharp-tailed grouse leaped in confused flurries. Steve pointed at a face-off of three grouse just as the birds lifted into the air, their white-tipped tails open above the sage. After the trio descended, they bowed to each other, kicking off a sequence of display. Their movements appeared stiff, but the sounds were wild. Hollow stomps boomed through the earth. Insectlike twitters rose in pitch to a screaming chorus. Each burst of wing whirring made me start in surprise. With set, expansive postures, the grouse inflated their purple neck sacs and whoofed air out with a rush. Then their formal courtship gestures exploded into a frenzy of pure dance.

One of the birds turned to bow deeply, head touching the ground, and another mounted squarely on its back. A simple touch completed the copulation, and the frenzy resumed. Unearthly cackles echoed from the basin as the sun's first rays flashed above the flat eastern horizon.

I heard a sudden whoosh of air off wings and reached out to warn Steve just as a raptor shot in from behind us. Long in the wings and moving fast, the prairie falcon stooped on the center of the lek. It broke through one tight group of dancing grouse, scattering them like ninepins across the hollow. When the falcon pulled up to clear the sagebrush on the far side of the basin, its talons were empty.

Steve and I stood up together as the prairie falcon sailed away into the sunlight. We were both opening our mouths to speak when fresh whoofs and stomps interrupted. The crowd of sharp-tails, missing only one beat, had returned to their dance. We settled back to our knees to watch the festivities within the grassy bowl.

THE OPPORTUNIST

I PLUNGED OFF THE BENCH BELOW PURPLE
Flat Top, headed for Chewelah Creek. The loose
glacial till made it easy to leap down the steep hillside
in long gliding footsteps, plowing past scarlet gilia and bluebells, flailing at the taller stalks of weedy yellow mullein and
toadflax, churning up a smell of rock dust and vanilla bark
that hung in the air for delicious minutes. It was a dash I had
made a thousand times, especially in late summer, headed as
now for shady pools too cold to flop in for more than an
instant. But on this particular afternoon, I slid to a stop
halfway down the hillside. Something wasn't right.

Instead of the fuzzy brush of mullein leaves against my
knees, something sharp raked at my legs with every step. The
culprit turned out to be a tall raggedy weed topped off by a
tight flowerhead. When I looked around the hillside, the
plant was everywhere, especially along the paths Tom and I

had worn into the slope. Some still bloomed with dull, white composite flowers, open candelabra crowned with dozens of small creamy blossoms like tufts of white flame. Bending down close, I could see beneath each flower a mosaic of pointed bracts, each tipped with a spine just stiff enough and long enough to deliver a sharp nip.

At the bottom of its stalk, a rosette of green leaves hugged the ground. Some of the whorls looked fresh, as if they had just germinated in the August heat; others seemed to have been around a while. I leaned down to finger the stalk of the nearest sprout and wrenched it up. It didn't give way easily, but I was stronger, and after a few rough tugs a long gnarly taproot emerged from the loose soil. I bent over and pulled another, and another, cursing under my breath if a stem broke off at the ground, drooling with satisfaction whenever a whole system tore loose in a shower of sand and fine glacial powder. Within fifteen minutes I had a small windrow piled on the slope. When I absently licked my fingers, they had an unusual taste—bitter, like a hard pill of quinine—which lingered on my tongue through supper. I returned to the slope at dusk, my trusty *Weeds of Eastern Washington* in hand, and identified the newcomer as *Centaurea diffusa*, diffuse knapweed.

Diffuse knapweed belongs to the complex Old World genus of *Centaurea*, kin to familiar ornamentals like bachelor's buttons and basketflower. Maddeningly adaptable, this species has been recorded at sites that receive anywhere from six to thirty-six inches of moisture a year. Knapweed begins its life as a ground-hugging whorl of divided leaves called a rosette, then sprouts upward into a branched, woody stalk. Every bit of the plant, from rosette to sepal, contains a chemical inhibitor which keeps other vegetation from invading its territory and is the source of that acrid quinine taste. In late summer the stalks produce dozens of many-petaled flowers, each of which disperses hundreds of seeds. The brittle skeletons of the mature plants persist for several years, and the rosettes send out adventitious roots that spread the colony outward in clumps.

Diffuse knapweed is native to Eurasia, ranging from the Balkans northeast to the Ukraine. It was first recorded in the United States in 1907 near Klickitat, along the Columbia Gorge; botanists thought that a few seeds must have come over mixed with hay seed from the Russian steppe. The plant had little trouble adapting to its new home; by 1931 a knapweed colony was flourishing along the rapids at The Dalles, that traditional meeting place of cultures. From there the irksome weed spread steadily across the dry open country east of the Cascades. At home I watched it overrun the abandoned city dump, outcompeting mullein, thistles, and sweet clover, then march up our driveway and along the creek bottoms like the multiplying brooms of the sorcerer's apprentice.

Wherever I traveled in the Inland Northwest, I found myself retracing the Centaurean invasion, until knapweed grew into a sort of regional symbol for me. While I was repelled by the plant's incursion, at the same time I found myself attracted to its power: There was its heritage on the steppe, which I had always imagined as Europe's analog to the open spaces of the American West. There was its opportunistic, almost fluid movement over disturbed land—its seedlings followed everything from log skidder tracks to the threads of gopher tunnels as the weed colonized distant hillsides in a few seasons' time. And most of all, there was the way the plant's steady immigration grated against the will of people. Knapweed was in the process of redefining a vast landscape, and I found plenty of soldiers lined up to fight for their territory.

I talked with a dedicated rancher who kept his place pristine by carrying a spray can of Tordon on his back. An amateur botanist insisted that poisons didn't give the native plants a chance to fight back against the invader. A mowing advocate told me that two good passes, in spring and late summer, cut the life out of the knapweed, but a dissenter showed me a study plot where mowing appeared to have spread the low rosettes at an alarming rate. I watched an entomologist test Eurasian gall-making wasps and root-boring beetles as biological controls, and met a biochemist who was experimenting with genetic mutation. I listened to a county agent implore participants at a pow wow to clean out their wheel wells, so that they wouldn't unwittingly carry seed from reservation to reservation. I commiserated with another agent who had given up the knapweed problem as hopeless, opting instead to concentrate his efforts against a more recent invasion of leafy spurge. I attended a conference where the whole future of eastern Montana rangeland was brought into question, and read a guidebook that listed ten more *Centaurea* species that were poised to spread through the Inland Northwest.

By this time I had glued a bumper sticker on my truck that pictured a knapweed plant beneath the legend WANTED: DEAD, and discovered that I couldn't pass a stand of the invaders without bending to pull some up. Many nights I went to sleep with the acrid taste of quinine on my lips, and the uneasy feeling that not only was this introduced weed usurping the habitat of some of my favorite wildflowers, but it was also driving reasonable people right out of their minds.

When I traveled from Spokane into western Montana the next July, I saw a different kind of knapweed—bigger, more persistent, with purple flowers. Called spotted knapweed, this species came ashore in British Columbia over a hundred years ago and outflanked its diffuse cousin by curling east, then south. Around the Idaho panhandle spotted and diffuse knapweed met, interbred, and took off in new directions.

When I arrived in Missoula, spotted knapweed was just beginning to bloom on the surrounding hillsides. Its purple glow outshone the pink of cheatgrass and the yellow-green of leafy spurge. Along Mount Jumbo's long saddle and rounded hilltop, where big ears of arrowleaf balsamroot should have dominated the scene, last year's knapweed stalks glistened with the silvery patina of aged wood. A friend of mine, tired of listening to my complaints, pointed me toward a plant-loving neighbor of hers who lived at the foot of Mount Jumbo, right inside the battle zone. His name was Klaus Lackshewitz.

"That's *Lock*-shave-itz," she said. "He likes for people to get it right."

We met under a European chokecherry tree in a flower garden that rambled along the front of Klaus's split-level house. He shook off my compliments on his horticultural work, pishing through his thin lips.

"No," he said, quietly surveying his domain. "It's not like what it should be. To do it properly you have to be out here every day, a little bit every day, and this year I haven't been able to do that."

Klaus was pushing eighty, and his reedy body seemed more like visible music than a physical mass. Yet he had produced a wonderful garden. Like Klaus, it handed out occasional pincushion surprises of color and swelled subtly with buds of the next idea. As he toured me through years of inspired collecting, a name would occasionally escape him, but he didn't seem to mind. His description of each plant was pure simplicity, even as he compared cuttings from southern Europe with natives of coastal British Columbia or measured a hybrid developed for its red bloom against the poppy named by his Latvian townsman Eschscholz. Everything seemed so well placed, the ratio of volume to space so perfect, that I had to wonder if the garden had lost anything over the past unusually rough winter.

"Some older plants, you know, that were uncomfortable in their environment, they passed on. But I don't think these that you see had any trouble."

The expression in his polished features was compassionate but not in the least sad. When I turned the subject to knapweed, he didn't recoil with the pursed lips I had grown so accustomed to seeing. He merely considered that one plant out of all the ones in his experience, seeming to recollect many different memories of it. His voice remained soft and musical when he spoke.

"Knapweed. How can I say it? It makes a wonderful dark honey, did you know that? I don't think I am feeling so threatened by that plant as some people."

It was a hundred-degree afternoon, and western Montana felt like the inside of a lumber drying kiln. We stepped through a doorway into a narrow hallway, papered with geological survey maps, which led to Klaus' study. Stacked neatly on his desk was his latest work: an annotated key to the plants of west-central Montana for the Forest Service. Three healthy piles of computer printouts lay on a table behind the desk. Among the artwork on the walls, my eyes were drawn to a small medieval scene, and Klaus walked over to tell its story. An Estonian, in traditional big robe and floppy hat, led four Christian knights on horseback. With their lances pointing straight up, they cradled a fallen comrade between them.

"Four times, you know," Klaus said. "Four times in the sixteenth century the Russians tried to overwhelm Latvia and Estonia. Each time, on the lake ice in the winter, the Teutonic knights drove them back."

Although Klaus was born and raised in Latvia, he did not call himself Latvian, but German Baltic—a testimony to

Germany's long-standing presence in the region. Our eyes moved from the sixteenth century on around the room. A narrow-brimmed schoolboy cap, with the Freemason's braided star, was the single possession he had retained from his homeland. He described Latvia as a land of icy muskegs, with moose browsing among stands of short willow and black spruce. There Klaus had developed an early passion for birds, and he remembered his favorite, a big reddish finch the Latvians called the Finnish parrot. He followed the winter birds until the region was caught up in the upheaval of World War II, and his family moved west to Germany.

"My father said when we left Latvia, he said, 'Always from now on we will be missing the plains and the sea.' "

Klaus was twenty-nine in 1940, the year he went into the German army. He marched into southern Russia, made it out, was captured in Poland late in the war, and spent two winters in a Russian prison camp. When he returned to the ruined countryside of Germany after his release, he found it sprouting purple with asters, as if the Allies had bombed the nation with seeds.

In 1952, while Klaus was still living in Germany, a sponsor approached him to refurbish an abandoned farm in Morristown, New Jersey. He arrived in the New World, not speaking a word of English, to find the farm in terrible shape. The first book he bought was a Peterson's bird guide, the second a local flora. In time, his wife, Gertrude, landed a job teaching German at the University of Montana, and they moved to Missoula. Klaus worked as a gardener at a nursery, then at the university herbarium.

"One day I asked a professor about a certain odd heather up on Lolo Pass—'Did it do this? Did it do that?' and the man shrugged and said 'Could be.' And I thought, my god, a scientist, who looks at these hills all the time—how can he not want to know?"

A botanist at the herbarium, impressed by the range of
Klaus's knowledge, signed him on as a plant collector. Klaus
hiked up into the Bitterroot Range, among the heathers and
Finnish parrots, which Westerners call pine grosbeaks. Until
a recent illness, he had remained with the plants ever since.

"Taxonomy is what I suppose I do," he said. "But I'm
really more of an explorer than a scientist."

We worked our way upstairs, where Gertrude had set out
tea: a yellow herbal remedy for Klaus, lavender for the two of
us. Our conversation drifted back to Germany and World
War II. Down in his study, Klaus had glossed over his military
career with a few quick words, but now, with Gertrude's
encouragement and a little help from a historical atlas, he
laid out a circuitous journey around eastern Europe.

His company had marched out of southern Poland in
1942, and met little resistance for a long time—his fingers
fought to find the names of the obliterated towns and tribu-
taries that marked their route. They had crossed the Dnieper
River and were moving for the Don, north of Crimea, in the
western Ukraine.

"There," Klaus touched an empty space on the chart.
"There I saw my first wolf. Two of us slept in a truck, away
from the troops. We had parked in the night you see, not
knowing where we were. And in the morning I opened my
eyes to see a wolf there running, forth and back, forth and
back, watching us all the time. With it were some ravens.
Always the ravens and wolves were following the Russian
army. From then on, they were treating our camps to their
music each night."

It was open country, dry and flat, without relief of any
kind except—and here Klaus molded his hands into the
shape of strange hummocks—except for the burial mounds of
Scythian nomads, invaders who in ancient times had wandered across central Asia into Europe. In those mounded

tombs, the Scythians buried fine artifacts depicting the fauna of their far-reaching travels, from leopard buckles to little golden bees.

As his own army moved toward the Don River, Klaus began to see beebirds of yellow and bluish green, which always perched with their recurved bills pointed straight up. The Russians called them *shchurka*, a word that mimicked the bird's two-noted call. Just as exotic to a traveler from the north was the rose-colored starling, ivory white with a black bridle and blush-tinted face. Klaus remembered a few small grain fields and some livestock, not much.

"Beautiful artemesias dominated the plant community, sage family members, not woody like the desert ones here, but leafy—a pretty green one, a pretty silver one . . . and then the patchy purple blossoms of knapweed, they are beginning. Little clumps, quite pleasant."

Klaus's company crossed the Don and failed at Stalingrad, then turned south and marched all the way to Armavir at the foot of the vast Caucacus Mountains. Knapweed stayed with them into the foothills, where the Russian army steadily encircled their invading force. Although Klaus made it safely back to Poland on the last troop train, he was captured soon afterward.

"But I don't want to be talking about that." With his delicate fingers, he flopped the thick atlas closed, and the splatter of unfamiliar names disappeared. "You have seen my front garden, where I keep my pretty herbs. Now shall we visit the wild plantings I am growing in the back?"

The slope of Mount Jumbo ascended straight off the slate patio behind Klaus's house. Beyond the property line, orange-barked yellow pines walked up the hill. They were spaced far enough apart to allow direct sunlight to the ground, and specimens of knapweed—many showing off their soft purple blooms—appeared everywhere there wasn't shade. Klaus owned an acre of this transition zone, which he had tailored by hand-pulling the knap and letting various other opportunists creep back in. There were bluebells and gilia, sticky geranium, goatsbeard, and rough fescue. A viny wild rose crowded an out-of-place domestic rosebush, and jags of quack grass ran through solid clumps of pinegrass.

"Different things will come in, and others will cycle out," said Klaus. "This is a good slope. There was a range scientist down at the university; he's gone now, but always he was saying: 'On the one hand . . . on the other hand . . . . See?'"

And here Klaus held out one palm, as if full of knowledge, then balanced the other against it, laughing the difference into insignificance. "On the one hand . . . on the other hand . . . . See?"

I took the opportunity to try him on the concept of using insects or genetic mutations against the aggression of a plant like knapweed.

"I don't have a scientific hold on it—but there's something . . . I don't have the word for it." As Klaus searched, a calliope hummingbird buzzed a feeder above the table; he watched it for a moment, then cocked an ear to listen to the birds of late afternoon.

"The ravens should be here soon. Then we'll have all kinds of different music." Standing on his slate patio, he listened some more.

"You remind me of chicory. Do you call it succory, or blue sailors? No one knows exactly where this plant came from— eastern Mediterranean, I suppose. When the railroad lines went through Europe in the nineteenth century, chicory spread from Spain to Siberia, and the people started calling it the road warden. There was a song about it: 'Wegewarte,' 'Road Warden.' It became quite a popular folk song in the early 1900s. The man who wrote it was killed in the first war.

How did that song go? 'Wegewarte, wegewarte . . .' I can't have the words."

Klaus coughed a couple of times, the furnace heat of the afternoon finally getting to his lungs. Gertrude materialized to constrain him. "You've been out long enough, Klaus, I think." As she ushered him back indoors, Klaus hummed his scrap of tune.

"Wegewarte, wegewarte. Road warden, road warden."

EARTH PEOPLE

*T*HE LIGHT HAZE ABOVE THE COLVILLE
Valley thickened as I rolled south through Springdale, heading over to the Spokane Reservation for
a meeting with Pauline Pascal Flett. This was the time of year
that the dust from fall farmwork blew up from the wheat
country, but the color and thickness of today's haze signified
something more—perhaps a grass fire out on the reservation
rangeland. A few days before, I had been picking up straw
bales with Lynn Walker when he hauled off and stomped his
foot hard in his field of stubble, then listened to a hollow
echo ring through the earth. "Watch out," he warned omi-
nously. "Weather stays this dry, we'll be looking at snow on
the dust."

As I cruised through the trading post at Ford and turned
west to cross the reservation boundary, it was hard to imagine
snow ever falling on anything but dust in this part of the

county. The summer sun had utterly parched this wedge between the Spokane and Columbia Rivers, burning into the open golden hills a raw appeal quite different from the valley where I lived. In earlier times, this place had bristled with healthy bunchgrass and the cackles of sharp-tailed grouse, but now a flood of prickly knapweed, still blooming white, followed the roadside and spilled far out into fields.

I passed the privately owned Smoke Shack, almost hidden by a thicket of wildly lettered signs announcing good deals on cigarettes and firecrackers. Off to the right a historical marker explained that a modest white wooden building had been the first Catholic church in the area, constructed a century before by Indians and missionaries. Farther on lay the sprawl of buildings that represented the Spokane tribe's post-and-pole business; beyond the end of the last conveyor, a chip pile bloomed with the milky mauve of mildew.

On the outskirts of Wellpinit, a double-trailered dump truck roared past, carrying raw ore from the uranium pit west of Wellpinit to the processing plant at Ford. A tornado of fine gray dust swirled off the cab and both trailers. As the cloud cleared I could see a large banner draped across the highway: WELCOME TO THE LARGEST NATIVE AMERICAN POW WOW IN THE INLAND NORTHWEST. That had been last weekend, and the huge parking lot and dance areas were completely empty now. A mile beyond the festival grounds, the Bureau of Indian Affairs complex looked almost as quiet.

Pauline's office was in the back of a sea-foam Quonset hut, beyond a random arrangement of empty desks and green partitions. The air above the painted concrete floor concentrated the day's hot, smoky weight. Old fluorescent lights winked through the dust, and quiet twangs of country music emanated from an unseen radio. Pauline's door stood slightly ajar, and I peeked inside to see her slumped over her desk, breathing easily. The red light of her tape recorder glowed beside her. Earphones and pencil lay poised on her desk, and beside her chair a box overflowed with cassettes. Two blackboards on the wall were covered with strangely accented script—phonetic spellings of the Spokane language.

"I'm not asleep," Pauline said suddenly, bobbing up to show her handsome face behind large glasses. Her voice was a little scratchy, but she did indeed look awake. She tapped at the red light on her machine.

"I just got stuck in the middle of one of Mom's tapes. Sometimes she talks so fast, I get all balled up trying to listen and write at the same time."

Pauline had spent the summer teaching Spokane to a class of young tribal members. Along with the basics of the language, she was trying to incorporate the oral history and legends she had been collecting from tribal elders. She pointed to her box of cassettes.

"Hearing these stories makes such a difference to the kids, but I've got a long way to go to get them transcribed."

Pauline's aim was to preserve as much of her tribal heritage as possible through the familiar tales that everyone had once known, told the way they had always been told. She also had plans for a usable dictionary for her classes and a comprehensive catalogue of local plants and animals. I had been helping her identify the animals and birds that appeared on her various tapes, and now she pulled out loose sheets of natural history information, rattling off names in Spokane with mellifluous twists and glottal stops until her voice wavered and then faded away.

"By the way," she whispered, beating her sternum to help her voice. "How come you never made it to Pow Wow?"

"Got hung up in Chewelah," I said lamely.

Pauline made Pow Wow sound like a dandy celebration. It attracted people from surrounding groups of Colville, Kalispel, Kootenai, Salish, Flathead, Nez Perce, Umatilla, and Yakima. Many others came from reservations farther away—Skokomish from the Olympic Peninsula, Blackfeet from across the Rockies, Paiute from southern Oregon and Nevada. There were dances and demonstrations by the best in their disciplines. Trade booths supplied goods from a multitude of cultures. Pauline herself spent the bulk of the weekend singing for the stick game, just as she had at every Pow Wow since she was a young girl. This was a family affair, and as a child Pauline and her siblings sang to help their father visualize which opponent's hand held the gaming stick. Since his death five years before, the family had not fared too well at the Pow Wows.

This past weekend had begun in much the same fashion, Pauline said. After the first few hours, they were down to their last stick. One more loss would put them out of the game, and Pauline had run through most of the family's repertoire of songs without success. Then on the final throw she heard her younger brother mouth the words of their father's special fawn song.

"Dad's song," Pauline repeated. "Brother's idea. It always brought good luck to Dad, you know. The fawn was his special power. None of us kids had used it for these past five seasons since he left us, because we were taught that kind of respect. But when my brother started singing Dad's song this weekend, we saw that it was from deep respect."

Following her brother's lead, Pauline had picked up the cadence of the fawn song. Singing straight through the long movement, they both remembered all the times their dad had led the song, and on the next point her brother guessed right. They kept repeating the song as he won back all their original sticks with an uncanny knowledge of his opponent's hand. Still following her brother, Pauline kept going until the family team had picked up every one of their rivals' sticks without a miss.

After that victory Pauline sang for a night and a day, keeping her voice strong with the cured root of a plant that she pronounced like a whisper from a raspy voice: *xasxs* according to her spelling, although a windy "whaswhs" was as close as I could come. From a pouch hidden in the depths of her purse, she handed me the thin rhizomic root tip of a lovage family plant. One nibble gave off a biting menthol taste—"bitter to you, but just right to me," Pauline smiled.

The traditional *xasxs* gathering grounds for the Spokane tribe were high, marshy areas on two mountains to the east. Pauline described the way she and her mother would remove the main root with a digging stick, then work up the smaller tendrils by hand. After pulling up a plant, they always replaced the broken stem with a prayer of thanks. Then they dried the roots in a special pouch such as the one hidden in Pauline's purse. After the proper curing period, they were used for a variety of purposes. A chunk might be hung within a baby's crib to prevent colds, or smoke from the burning root blown onto a victim of spirit possession. No singer would think of going to a stick game without a good supply of *xasxs*, Pauline said, finishing her sentence above the persistent ring of the telephone.

While she was on the phone, I went over her latest lists of Spokane names for local flora and fauna. I couldn't help but overhear bits of the conversation, and Pauline was steaming when she hung up. A grant that she had felt sure the Language Center would get had not come through. The new school term was beginning on the reservation, and she didn't have the right materials ready to help the children learn about themselves. This phone call meant it would be at least another year before she would have any more funds for her story transcription project, and several of her best sources within the tribe were growing old.

Pauline took off her glasses and rubbed her eyes. "You know, we never would have gotten anywhere on this if we'd spent all our time waiting for the next grant to come through. Let's go ahead and try to make some sense out of these names."

I pulled out the lists I had prepared of all the birds, mammals, reptiles, and fish that should occur on the Spokane Reservation. As she read off several Spokane names for birds that she had gleaned from her mother's stories, I recognized the peculiar diving wing sound of the common nighthawk: *sbas* in Spokane. But most of the unknown words slipped by, and there was no escaping the fact that to really contribute to this project I would have to learn the Spokane language. Pauline produced a beginner's pronunciation tape, but warned me that for some reason it was very hard for a white person to ever pick up much Spokane.

"It's no small deal either," she continued. "We need to know the whole language, so we can get each of the stories told exactly right. Otherwise, they don't carry all their meaning."

I gathered up my lists and made ready to leave. Pauline ejected the cassette tape that was in her recorder, flipped it over, punched it back in, and hung the earphones over her neck.

"There's so much to do," she said. "And so many paths that don't even make a beginning."

Out again in the open country, smoke from the range fire appeared to be thinning. Just past the abandoned school-house at Ford I stopped beside a refrigerator-sized stone marker. Shaped from a piece of local granite, its rough-hewn surface was dotted with yellow and gray-black lichens that framed the message on its polished face.

COMMEMORATING THE ESTABLISHING
OF A MISSION AMONG THE SPOKANE INDIANS
ON THESE GROUNDS BY THE REVERENDS
CUSHING EELLS AND ELKANAH WALKER
FROM SEPT. 1838 TO MAR. 1848
TSHIMAKAIN
ON THIS SPOT STOOD THE EELLS HOME
ERECTED BY
THE STATE HISTORICAL SOCIETY AND
THE CONGREGATIONAL CHURCHES
OF WASHINGTON

More chiseled letters lined the sides of the marker. The left side detailed the dates of Cushing Eells, his long-suffering wife, Myra, and their two children born on the site. Elkanah Walker's dates were laid into the right side of the stone, along with those of his wife, Mary Richardson Walker, and the five children she produced here: BORN TSHIMAKAIN.

After journeying west across the plains with her new husband, Mary Walker arrived at Tshimakain to set up house in a small log hut. Her diaries and letters detail the nine years she spent at the mission, a life in which missionary zeal gave ground to the simple, grinding chores of subsistence: on a single February day in 1841, Mary "ironed, starched clothes & mended chimney once more, tho I had designed not to do it. Got very tired . . . Got into trouble with some lice." On other days she figured out how to make mincemeat pies without apples and nursed pumpkins and cucumbers through the short growing season. She fought off the wild dogs that looted the camps and listened to wolves howling close by at night. She watched her best cow die from eating a wild poisonous plant and stewed local lily roots brought in by the Spokane chief she called Cornelius. She constantly studied the natural history of the area, impressing visitors with the depth of her knowledge.

Mary Walker's life in Tshimakain was also full of more complex questions of understanding and soul. She tried to teach the Spokane people something of her outside world— "I gave them a lesson in geography on an egg shell which I had painted for a globe"—even as she absorbed pieces of theirs: "Listened till I was half amazed today to an old woman who attempted to make me understand their method of computing time. I got ten divisions of the day, the changes of the moon & its name."

Mary chastised herself for being slow to translate Christian hymns so the Spokanes would have something to sing as Elkanah preached. She cringed when Catholic priests like Father De Smet visited Fort Colville, agreeing with Elkanah that the Congregationalists had first claim on the territory. She worried about smacking her two-year old boy, Cyrus, when he acted contrary. She tried, sometimes unsuccessfully, to swallow complaints against her cohorts, the Eells: "Meet with a great deal in Mr. E to vex & try me . . . . Mrs. E. heart sick about my talk to her yesterday."

Mary also fought hard against her own perceived weaknesses and smoldered at the regular rebukes of the moody Elkanah: "Have felt the past week several times as if I could no longer endure certain things that I find in my husband." But Mary did endure these things, sticking with Elkanah and the Eells and the mission for nine years. During that time, the missionaries did not baptize a single convert, nor did they succeed in convincing the Spokanes to give up their seasonal movements, their preference for roots and salmon over wheat and potatoes, or their reliance on traditional medicine rites. Yet, despite their frustrations, the missionaries lived on friendly terms with the Spokanes, and left the place they had come to call home only with great reluctance during the height of the Cayuse War. "Feel very sad about leaving, but feel on the whole it is safest . . . . We left home at noon, perhaps to return no more. It commenced raining as we left."

At the base of the monument, a single mariposa lily graced a spot of raw dirt. The flower took the form of a tulip-sized bloom atop a leafless, unbranched stem; only eight inches tall, it blended right in with the gravel of the roadside. I knelt down to touch it, tough leathery petals seamed together into a lavender cup. Inside, stripes of deeper purple surrounded a bright yellow sunburst coated with a layer of fine gray dust.

Across a fenceless field from the granite marker stood a charred pine snag. The yellow pine grew huge around its base, but at head height the butt split into several upright trunks, each one twisted orange and black. Beyond it I could see lines of the bright green trees that thrive around water in dry country—willows, hawthorns, chokecherries, alder— and I wandered toward the moisture. From a distance the lush trees promised burbling streams, but the first channel I walked into ran only with sand and gravel. Beside the leaves of last spring's camas lilies, tough sprouts of pungent sage lined the watercourse. Although a flood line of debris marked each bush halfway up, a quarter-mile walk revealed not a single puddle. I touched the bushes on the bank, brushing back inch-long hawthorn briars and knobby alder catkins before snapping off a green willow stick perhaps a yard long. I balanced the twig between thumb and forefinger and headed for the next line of trees, hoping for a drink of cool water.